The Ta'mar Spirit
The righteous shall flourish like the palm tree... Psalm 92:12a

8-28-11

To Ramona,
A bold spirit for Christ.
Yet you are gentle and humble.
God is getting ready to lead
and guide like never before.
You shall flourish like
the palm tree. You
are Victorious!

Love,
Sophia

1

Dedication

This book is dedicated to my loving parents for believing in me and supporting me in all my endeavors. Thanks for continuing to pray, encourage, and guide me through it all. I even appreciate all the "meetings" we have brainstorming our visions to be God's entrepreneurs. (Smiles) Also, to my biological mother who is deceased; however, her legacy still remains alive. As I mature I understand more and more all those lessons she taught me while she was alive. Her wisdom has helped to mold me.

To my family who continues to lift me up before God in prayer. I cherish the close bond we have and the memories we continue to create together.

A special thank you to Joy S., Melissa L., Tamara J., Mary J., Katrina M., Ashari S., Inzlea M., and Ronnal M. Thank you for all of your input and support in helping me to birth this book forward.

I love you all and I appreciate each of you being in my corner cheering for me. Thank you all for being my cheering squad.

Table of Contents

Preface

Once, while I was at the highest point in the city, I looked out to see all of God's amazing creations. What I saw and comprehended will pale in comparison to the words I will attempt to describe the sight.

The horizon met the land and there was no beginning or end. It was as if every little thing depended on the next to survive; perfect harmony. The awesome masterpiece that stretched out before me was breathtakingly beautiful. The clouds appeared to be painted in the sky by a master artist whose hands had been steadied through the years. They were flawless. The sky was clear blue.

As I looked up and saw the winged creatures soar through the sky, I began to get emotional. I wanted to be like those creatures; Going through life without a care in the world. They were at peace soaring above the hustle and bustle beneath. They were so tiny in that sea of blue, but it didn't seem to phase them. They knew where their strength lay and, therefore, the sky was limitless.

I did not want to worry any more. I did not want to take matters into my own hands. I needed to know and experience God being my provider. I needed the peace of God to inundate me. I wanted the Lord's blessings to overtake me so that I could cast all of my cares upon Him. I sought peace beyond all understanding – The peace that would calm me before, during, and after the storm.

The land had a foggy majestic appeal to it. On each side of me was a major highway that I could follow as far as the eyes would allow. In all directions was more magnificent beauty. North, South, East, and West, they all took you to God's wonderment. Every direction was paved with the peace of the Almighty.

Think of life and how good God has been. Give the Father His due reverence. Through the ups and downs, if you would ... could only be still and listen, you would ... could grasp the lessons being taught, the growth taking place in your life. He is truly an awesome and wonderful God and He desires that you rest in Him because He is your peace.

With these words of inspiration, I hope this book gives you the strength to go through the day with your head held high no matter what obstacles may come your way. May the Peace of God always be with you.

Chapter 1

Journey towards Peace

Wherefore say, Behold, I give unto him my covenant of peace: And he shall have it, and his seed after him, even the covenant of an everlasting priesthood; because he was zealous for his God... Numbers 25:12, 13 KJV

I have been unstable at various points in my life but I purposed that with everything that was stable in my life I would live for Jesus. I was comfortable just going to church and occupying the pew. I was at ease with listening but not taking heed and applying the matters of God to my life. One day, I got tired. One day, I became stable and realized that my world was rocky.

This has been a journey. It has taken years to progress to where I am now. I am no longer comfortable with living a haphazard life for God. I desire to do and be more in Jesus Christ because I believe that I CAN DO ALL THINGS THROUGH CHRIST. I believe He strengthens me.

I am thankful to God that He saw fit to birth a precious Word through me. God gave me this creed to live by: Be Humble or Be Humiliated. I choose to be humble at the feet of Jesus. I choose to be saved, living a Holy life. I choose to renew my mind daily. I choose to believe that I am healed from infirmities. I choose to believe that there is good and evil present. Therefore, I believe that I must be on guard at all times.

The time is now pressing for all to "work out your own salvation with fear and trembling," according to Philippians 2:12. We must become aware of negative strongholds that are gripping our lives.

Unleash a never before felt anointing in your life. Declare and decreed it to be so. God is speaking to whomever will hear the clarion call. Transport unseen to seen. God is the inspirational force that will cause change in your life. God is not so deep that you cannot understand Him.

Our intellects cause us to over think and over analyze the nature of God. By over thinking and over analyzing, we underestimate the potency of God. We believe that God cannot save, deliver, and set us free from whatever has a grip on us. We believe our issues are too hard for God. We believe we are not worthy to be saved. However, God shows us every single second how worthy we are. His methods of delivery vary from circumstance to circumstance and from person to person. God will tailor-make your journey to peace, salvation, deliverance, and more.

In certain situations we benefit by learning from examples. If we could just apply God in our lives like those who overcome obstacles, we know we can make it. By first taking the Word of God and then seeing God's Word expressly used in the lives of REAL men and women. We glean hope and courage. We grow in knowledge. Not just any random knowledge but God's knowledge. We grow in wisdom; not worldly wisdom but Godly wisdom. We grow in understanding; not self understanding but Godly understanding. We become erect in our ways of thinking, talking, and living. We stand in the midst of trials and tribulations because we understand that God is the author of the storm. With all of this, we ultimately possess the peace of God. The peace that allows us to go through storms firmly planted in the Word of God by the Spirit of God.

Storms are part of life. We cannot avoid them. God desires to elevate our mindsets so that we STAND and believe that He can sustain us. Once our mindsets are changed, our lives are changed. Once our lives are changed, our standards change. When our standards change, we require more. Upon requiring more we place greater demands on life and the people around us. If these people do not line up, we are to be the light that draws them to Jesus so that He can bring them into Holy and Righteous alignment. We also begin to place greater demands on God and the Holy Spirit. We should never again return to the place of complacency or unrest. Peace should become part of our lifestyles because surely goodness and mercy follow us all the days of our lives. We dwell in the house of the Lord!

When you wash clothes does the washing machine stand still? No, there is agitation. The movement of the drum is what forces the clothes to go back and forth causing dirt and grime to be removed. We have to become as washing machines. We have to move according to the Word of God so that our lives can be cleaned by Him. God is the machine, He is the detergent, He is the water, and He is every setting on the machine. In other words, God knows what it will take for each of us to be pure and Holy, living clean lives. He knows just how to bring out His peace within us. This is why His Word tells us to present our bodies as living sacrifices, Holy and acceptable. It is our reasonable service. If your current service to God is plagued with unrighteousness, then it is time for you to come clean.

If you are bent out of shape by unhealthy living, then it is time to stand erect. If your sense of accountability is perverted, you need to be renewed. If your sense of right and wrong has morphed into a belief system more suited for worldly living, become like the prodigal son and return to the Father. God will change you. He will purge you and wash you. His blood will purify you beyond measure. Try Jesus His peace awaits you!

I thank God that when I was deep in my sins there were saints that knew Jesus. They prayed me through. They cried out on my behalf. The prayers of the righteous availed much. When you know and apply the Word of God to your life, His Word becomes sharper than any two edge sword. God is a man of war. The battle is fixed and you are already victorious. The peace of God is yours for the taking.

This is about exposure and release. The goal is to get issues and situations out in the open. If you keep a bandage on a wound so that it is not allowed to breathe, it will never heal. At some point, you have to pull the bandage off. Allow the Holy Spirit to breathe new life into you. May the Holy Spirit of our precious Lord and Saviour breathe on you right now!

Chapter 2

Who Is Ta'mar?

For wisdom will enter your heart, and knowledge will be pleasant to your soul. Discretion will protect you, and understanding will guard you. Wisdom will save you from the ways of wicked men, from men whose words are perverse... Proverbs 2:10-12 NIV

II Samuel 13:1-6

> ¹After this Ab'salom the son of Da'vid had a lovely sister, whose name *was* Ta'mar; and Am'non the son of Da'vid loved her. ² Am'non was so distressed over his sister Ta'mar that he became sick; for she *was* a virgin. And it was improper for Am'non to do anything to her. ³ But Am'non had a friend whose name *was* Jon'adab the son of Shim'eah, Da'vid's brother. Now Jon'adab *was* a very crafty man. ⁴ And he said to him, "Why *are* you, the king's son, becoming thinner day after day? Will you not tell me?"Am'non said to him, "I love Ta'mar, my brother Ab'salom's sister." ⁵ So Jon'adab said to him, "Lie down on your bed and pretend to be ill. And when your father comes to see you, say to him, 'Please let my sister Ta'mar come and give me food, and prepare the food in my sight, that I may see *it* and eat it from her hand.'" ⁶ Then Am'non lay down and pretended to be ill; and when the king came to see him, Am'non said to the king, "Please let Ta'mar my sister come and make a couple of cakes for me in my sight, that I may eat from her hand.

Ah-ha! This is the beginning.   This is where all the trouble started. Am'non was sick, right?   On the contrary, this was the manifestation of Da'vid's folly.

Enter the first contributor, Am'non. Am'non visibly looked and seemed out of sorts. There wasn't a waking moment that his mind wasn't on the "object" of his affection.   There was one BIG problem though.   The "object" was his half sister, Ta'mar.   He loved her in a way that brothers ought not to love their sisters and vice versa. He lusted after her.

Am'non. His Hebrew name means "Faithful" or "True." **Faithful** means "loyal." **True** is defined as "real" or "genuine." It is impossible to deny Am'non his feelings.

Enter the second contributor, Jon'adab. The Bible states that he was a subtle or wise man. Jon'adab was cunning, crafty, wily, and shrewd. He noticed that Am'non was love struck. He also noticed that Am'non was getting slimmer which was a direct contradiction because Am'non was royalty and sat at the King's table. Royalty always ate well. So he decided to investigate the issue.

Jon'adab. His Hebrew name means "whom Jehovah impels" or "Jehovah is willing." **Impel** means "to drive or move forward."

Let's go back to verse two, "And Am'non was so vexed, that he fell sick for his sister Ta'mar; for she was a virgin; and Am'non thought it hard for him to do anything to her." This passage shows the difficulty Am'non had with wanting to be intimate with his sister and restraining himself. It appears that if Ta'mar was not a virgin then being with her would have been easier. He would have pursued her with no second thought regardless of her being his half sister. However, with a little coaxing by Jon'adab Am'non summoned the inner strength to pursue Ta'mar. At some point in their conversation, Am'non reasoned within himself that Jon'adab's advice was sound.

Ref: Song of Solomon 2:15

It doesn't take much convincing when a person wants something bad enough. In one conversation, Jon'adab supplied Am'non with enough confidence and "drive" to "move forward" to "have" Ta'mar. It became irrelevant that Ta'mar was a virgin. It also did not matter that she was his half sister; a blood relative.

At this juncture, realize that Am'non, as applied to your life, is gender free. The developing situation represents the enemy plotting to steal, kill, and destroy your life. The devil is a copycat

14

of God. God calls all to Him because He has no respect of person. We are all His children. The Lord desires to keep His children safe from hurt, harm, and danger. The devil also has no respect of person either. The enemy is gender neutral, lacks pigmentation, and is age old. Remember Ephesians 6:6-20. Whether male or female, the enemy will use anyone and anything (media outlets, and various other outlets) to destroy you. I Peter 5:8 states, "Be sober, be vigilant; because your adversary the devil, as a roaring lion, walketh about, seeking whom he may devour." The Bible declares that God from the beginning created man in His image; male and female created He them. God has a masculine and feminine side. It is important to know all sides of the Lord to be complete and whole in Him.

The Scripture says that Ta'mar was fair or beautiful. Am'non desired but knew he could not have this reputed beauty. His desire did not wane. If only Da'vid had shared his story about lust and the fruit of it with his offspring. If he only shared about reaping and sowing, then this situation or event would probably not have gone the way it did. Am'non would have fasted and prayed to remove the urges he felt towards his sister. He would have TOLD Jon'adab of his impure thoughts and, yet, he would have rebuked Jon'adab for trying to "drive" him to commit such a heinous act. However, the Bible does not share this event in that light. The Bible does not state that GOD himself stepped in to even warn or protect all partakers of the soon coming calamity. It does not even read that a prophet was sent forth to warn King Da'vid about the evil plans of Am'non, pushed by Jon'adab, towards Ta'mar. Instead, the set up was set in motion.

Ref: Proverbs 1:10

The Set Up

II Samuel 13:7-10

> **⁷And Da'vid sent home to Ta'mar, saying, "Now go to your brother Am'non's house, and prepare food for him."**
> **⁸ So Ta'mar went to her brother Am'non's house; and he**

was lying down. Then she took flour and kneaded *it,* made cakes in his sight, and baked the cakes. [9] And she took the pan and placed *them* out before him, but he refused to eat. Then Am'non said, "Have everyone go out from me." And they all went out from him. [10] Then Am'non said to Ta'mar, "Bring the food into the bedroom, that I may eat from your hand." And Ta'mar took the cakes which she had made, and brought *them* to Am'non her brother in the bedroom.

We now have the third and fourth contributors, King Da'vid and Ta'mar, respectively.

Da'vid means "well-beloved." He was appointed and anointed by God to be King of the children of Is'rael. Da'vid was the unsuspecting participant in Am'non's treachery; just like Uri'ah was in Da'vid's debauchery. In fact, Da'vid played a major role in the set up. He was the King. The King ordered Ta'mar to her brother's house.

According to Jewish customs, females lived separate from males. Yet, at some point, Am'non laid eyes on Ta'mar. He must have sensed the wholeness and purity exuding from her. Ta'mar was a virgin and virgins wore different raiment from women who were married. Am'non, it seems, wanted that pureness felt whenever he thought of Ta'mar. His feelings were misguided and warped into evil intentions.

Ta'mar. Her name means "date palm" or "palm tree." It is odd for her name to refer to such a seemingly insignificant piece of wood. The revelation will be explained later on about the powerful, Biblical significance of Ta'mar and its spiritual application.

Ta'mar should have seen this set up coming. She should have felt eerie or uncomfortable when her brother ordered everyone out of the room.

Remember, Am'non was vexed by feelings of love for his sister. He was "love sick." He could not eat. He was growing lean day by day. Anyone who looked at him saw and believed that he was sick from some unknown illness or disease.

Why did she follow him?

When you are a virgin you have pure thoughts and you trust. You have not been tainted by the world. No one has dealt harshly with you.

If you are familiar with the Scripture passage, then maybe your thoughts might have gone a little something like this; Lord have mercy. Father show me the meaning of this Scripture. Help me to learn from this. What lesson am I to take away from this?

Are your thoughts now going back to your "virginity" days? Virginity stems from virgin. Biblically speaking, **Virgin** means to "separate." The dictionary portrays **Virgin** as "untouched, unused, pure."

Unmarried daughters were isolated from the presence of ALL men, be it family or non-family, without being accompanied. The other implement is unmarried meant virgin. God wants you separated from the world so the "Am'non's" cannot lead you into the intimate chamber. Set ups have caused so many to experience the wrong kind of inner chamber experience.

Take a moment to think over your life and begin to write down all those times you were "set up" and led into the intimate chamber by the enemy. A blank sheet of paper has been included for you at the end of this chapter. Whether you were the cause of the set up or someone else was, it is time to face these situations. Later on in the book, points will be covered to aid in letting go of "set ups." For now, write them down.

Are feelings of anger, shame, denial, or peace surfacing? Be honest. One can never heal without honesty. There is no peace in denial.

Let's Pray…

FATHER GOD in the MIGHTY NAME OF JESUS, I come to You, my Lord and Saviour, asking for strength to face my "set ups" and all those times I was led into intimate chambers by the enemy. Holy Spirit I ask right now that You give me the strength to hand over these situations that have caused me to act, move, and operate outside of Your Will. I need You now God. As You carry my burdens, Lord cause me to feel lighter in my spirit man. Lord I thank You for purging me of the very issues that have been weighing me down. Lord I ask that You cover me as I expose myself to You. It is in Jesus' name I ask, Amen.

In the purest of states, trust is given without any second, third, or fourth guessing. No feelings of threat are exhibited towards a loved one. After all, it is family. Family looks after one another and protects one another, right? The REAL body of Christ's family does, but not followers of the Father of Lies. The enemy will use anyone who will allow themselves to be used. The enemy constantly attacks followers of Christ but because they resist him he flees from them. As soon as a person steps out of the Will of God, they become instant <u>vessels</u> to be used by Satan.

Ref: Revelation 12:9; I Corinthians 14:33; John 10:10

Right now, be grateful and thankful for "But God." God can turn any situation or circumstance around. God is Omnipotent! Staying in His Will guarantees that no matter what we go through, the trying of faith produces and yields pure gold.

Ref: Zechariah 13:9; I Samuel 22:31

Ta'mar did not waste any time going to tend to her brother. Once she arrived she immediately set out preparing his food. She didn't question at all. She trusted. She was pure and untouched by life. She had never experienced any circumstance that would teach her that life didn't play fair. She was faithful in looking after and taking care of her loved one.

There are two sides of God. A strong, powerful force to be reckoned with and a gentle, tender side that provides and nurtures. The Ta'mar Spirit takes us out of the gender state which is carnal by nature and leads us into the spiritual realm. This becomes important in grasping the in-depth spiritual meaning of this scripture passage. Whether male or female, we all have gentle, tender sides. We have all, at one point, gone through great lengths to care for those we cherish. We have all exposed ourselves to people to gain trust.

The Scripture gives a very descriptive picture of Ta'mar's preparation of the meat (food). She was cooking bread. Preparing fresh, made from scratch meals, especially bread is a process and takes time. There are two dynamics at play here. Am'non patiently waits to complete the "set up," ensuring all his ducks are in a row while Ta'mar tediously shows every step to her brother to reassure him that she isn't attempting to harm him. Remember Am'non did not want his servants to prepare his food. It is implied that there was a lack of trust in his servants to take care of him while he was sick. He wanted, needed family there. He wanted, needed someone whom he trusted to have his back.

Life illustrates some set ups will happen quickly while other set ups will take time to form. The truth is that the enemy knows you are destined for greatness. He is willing to wait for the right moment, the right opportunity to utterly destroy you. You are special to God and the enemy desires to attack and sift you as wheat.

Ref: Romans 8:28

The Hook, Line, and Sinker

II Samuel 13:11-15

> 11 Now when she had brought *them* to him to eat, he took hold of her and said to her, "Come, lie with me, my sister." 12 But she answered him, "No, my brother, do not force me, for no such thing should be done in Is'rael. Do not do this disgraceful thing [folly]! 13 And I, where could I take my shame? And as for you, you would be like one of the fools in Is'rael. Now therefore, please speak to the king; for he will not withhold me from you." 14 However, he would not heed her voice; and being stronger than

19

she, he forced her and lay with her. ¹⁵ Then Am'non hated her exceedingly, so that the hatred with which he hated her *was* greater than the love with which he had loved her. And Am'non said to her, "Arise, be gone!"

Food in hand, Ta'mar followed Am'non into the inner most chamber, the bedroom. Before she knew it, her brother grabbed her. He wanted her to lie with him. They had just made it through the inner chamber doors when he made his proclamation. He even referred to her as his sister. But a brother would not treat his sister that way. He earlier acknowledged to Jon'adab that she was "my brother's sister." Am'non denied the fact that Ta'mar was his sister. Now Ta'mar was there with him and he used their intimate relationship for manipulative purposes.

All words have meanings. The Bible declares that the word **Name** means "reputation." This statement seems very menial and insignificant. Everyone knows that words have meanings and meanings carry reputations. In Exodus, Moses is chosen by God to lead the children of Is'rael out of Egypt (bondage). Moses asked a question of the Lord, "whom should I say sent me?" The Lord responded, "I AM THAT I AM." I AM is powerful. I AM is positive. I AM is the powerful, positive persona of God Almighty. So why then do we call ourselves names outside of the scope of what Jesus calls us?

The enemy uses false sentiment to ensnare and mislead. Terms like dumb, stupid, pathetic, whore, dog, addict, thug, simple, bum, ignorant, are used outside of a believer's presence or earshot. But, the enemy uses all the deceptively, charming terms of endearment to make a believer's heart melt while he is in a believer's presence.

Ta'mar responded, "No, my brother" acknowledging the familial relationship. No such thing should be done in Is'rael. The Hebrew meaning of **Is'rael** is "God prevails." Ta'mar reminded Am'non that he should not do this because God would prevail. The enemy is already defeated because God always prevails. No matter how many rough patches, you have the victory. Keep making the statement that "God prevails" to all Am'nons that manifest.

This assault ought not to be committed because God will triumph. It does not matter the force that is experienced. Partakers of Glory in Christ are partakers of suffering as well. God prevails and remains Glorified.

Ref: Romans 8:17, 18

Ta'mar asked Am'non if he did this act where she would go because of the shame. She would lose her distinguishing characteristics of being separate and untouched. At his hands, she would thereafter put on different raiment because of his "force."

Because Am'non only thought of himself, Ta'mar attempted to appeal to him in another manner. She stated that if he did this folly, this foolishness, then he would become a fool like those in Is'rael. Ta'mar tried to implore Am'non by reminding him of his royal status. He was next in line for the kingdom. She reasoned with him that this was idiotic behavior. Ta'mar attempted to show Am'non that he would mess up his life if he forced her to do something that they both knew was wrong in the sight of God. Am'non did not take heed to Ta'mar's wisdom.

Ref: Proverbs 1:20-28

Am'non forced Ta'mar to lay with him. In today's society, we consider this rape! The word **Rape** originates from the Latin verb **Rapere** "to seize or take by force." The Latin term for the act of rape itself is **Raptus**. The word originally had no sexual connotation. **Force** means "to put or impose (something or someone) forcibly on or upon a person." What started out as innocent pining for something or someone that was untouchable and pure turned into a web of lies, fear, shame, grief, sorrow, and hatred. Why? Because Am'non imposed himself upon Ta'mar and he never tried to understand her position. One dimensional person's are selfish and never attempt to walk in another person's shoes. God knew this and so He sent His son Jesus to walk among His people, as an example, to show and prove He understood the dynamics of life. Jesus Christ endured many things at the hands of mankind. Yet, He was committed to going to the Cross for you and me.

Ta'mar suggested speaking to the King to make the conflict legit. Both Ta'mar and Am'non were probably aware of Leviticus 18:11, "The nakedness of thy father's wife's daughter, begotten of thy father, she is thy sister, thou shalt not uncover her nakedness."

There is some validation in the coin phrase, "thin line between love and hate." Am'non began with a love that was so strong for Ta'mar that he was distressed. He was so miserable that he was noticeably growing lean. Yet, after he succeeded with Jon'adab's plan, that love abruptly twisted into seething hatred. And now, he wants her gone!

We all have been in situations in which someone or something was imposed upon us. How or what we thought did not matter and was not even considered. We truly do not want to be part of a "set up," and fall for something "hook, line, and sinker" that will hurt us, even when we subject ourselves to situations that we know we shouldn't be associated with.

The enemy has forced you to "lay with" him due to a lack of not knowing the Father and who He truly is in your life. By not knowing who you are in the Father you could find yourself being "took hold of." It was phrased purposely as "took hold of" because your biological parents or those who raised you might not have warned or even taught you about all of the evil that exists in the world. You sometimes might have found yourself pleading with the enemy and the very enemy manifested as family. Sometimes the very ones you love are the ones that may have harmed you - forced you into situations that you may not want to admit today. Realize that evil seeds were planted and have caused you to act out of God's character. Dig up those roots through the Word of God and DESTROY them by the power of the blood of Jesus and infilling of the Holy Spirit because these evil seeds were designed to abort your destiny in Christ.

Ref: Genesis 3:15

As we live, we will come across many Am'non's and Jon'adab. Those like Am'non feign for us while those like Jon'adab plot the course to get to us. We soon find ourselves deeply entangled in deceit and betrayal; our virginity snatched from us. We never had a fighting chance because we trusted. This information is not aimed at preventing anyone from trusting. On the contrary, it is designed to inform you to stop trusting in the enemy. Recognize that the enemy is only here to "bruise your heel." The enemy desires your soul. Put all of your trust in Jesus Christ. He is the Seed sent that can and will bruise the enemy's head! It is by Jesus Christ's blood that we are cleansed and made whole.

Ref: Proverbs 3:5-8

How many times have we come across situations that caught us off guard? We tried to fight off attacks by stating that the situations were folly. When that didn't work, we made attempts of compromise. We even made great efforts to take situations to our Heavenly Father so that He could legitimize what was clearly outlawed or better yet sin.

We sometimes find ourselves in relationships and situations in which the very person, place, and/or activity we should not be with, around, or doing, shows us that they or it really does not like nor love us. We are being mistreated, lied to, lied on, abused mentally, physically, emotionally, and financially; the list goes on and on. We cannot seem to find our way out and we even begin to question if we really want to be free. We begin to live and embrace the lifestyle that brings instant gratification. Subsequently, we are so conditioned that we do not know how to retreat even in the midst of finding ourselves being rejected.

The Rejection

II Samuel 13:16-18

> 16 So she said to him, "No, indeed! This evil of sending me away *is* worse than the other that you did to me." But he would not listen to her. 17 Then he called his servant who attended him, and said, "Here! Put this *woman* out, away from me, and bolt the door behind her." 18 Now she

had on a robe of many colors, for the king's virgin daughters wore such apparel. And his servant put her out and bolted the door behind her.

After Am'non's imposition upon Ta'mar, he wanted her gone from his sight. She attempted to reason with him. Why did he want to throw her out now? She thought she was the object of his affection? Am'non has brought even more hurt and shame to Ta'mar. He had just treated her like she played the harlot. But Am'non ignored her and called for his servant he previously kicked out of the room to throw her out by "force." She was no longer his sister. Her title became "this woman." Am'non even instructed the servant to lock the doors just in case she tried to force her way back in to him. This was the allusion given in his instructions. Now Ta'mar was locked out, alone, in pain, suffering, and tainted. No longer would she wear the multi-colored robe adorned only by royal virgins.

The enemy will always reveal himself to you. The devil will call you all those names, to your face, that he called you behind your back. It is up to you to believe it. The enemy means you no good. To continually go back to the enemy reinforces the derogatory reputation the enemy uses to destroy you. Use your God given reputation instead. God sees you are His beloved. The enemy sees you are nothing to be loved. God sees you are extraordinary. The enemy sees you as less than ordinary. Whose report will you believe?

"Mankind's rejection is God's protection." The author of this quote is unknown but the impact of the words is powerful. Do not try to break back into the enemy's house to prove you are somebody. Beloved, do not waste your precious time. The enemy does not care. His mission was accomplished.

While searching your life and proceeding with this reality check, how many times have you encountered the enemy's impositions? Were there times when you recognized the "hook, line, and sinker" and yet other times you did not? Regardless of recognition, the end result was the same. You ended up locked out, feeling all alone, suffering from pain, and tainted. Feeling disqualified from being able to adorn royal apparel that all of the King's heirs are entitled to wear may have also arisen.

My brother and sister what are you wearing? Is it raiment of hurt and shame or anger from the past? It is time to shed those clothes! Put on the whole armor of God. It is never too late to discard those old garments and adorn new ones.

> To appoint unto them that mourn in Zion, to give unto them beauty for ashes, the oil of joy for mourning, the garment of praise for the spirit of heaviness; that they might be called <u>trees of righteousness, the planting of the LORD, that he might be glorified</u>. *Isaiah 61:3 KJV*

Confession

Intimate relations as well as masturbation were weaknesses. I struggled for years. I abstained and just like any unreformed addict, fell off the proverbial "wagon" time and time again. I prayed for relief from God. The prayer seemed to work for a while and then I fell again. Finally, I realized the problem wasn't my prayers but me. I played with the enemy concerning my weaknesses instead of shunning him completely. God showed me in a dream the true filthiness of my lifestyle. In the dream, I was getting ready for bed and pulled back the covers to discover black creepy, crawly bugs. Instead of killing the bugs and changing the linen and comforter, or even being disturbed by the sight, I pulled back the covers enough to avoid the bugs. God showed me my current condition. He revealed to me that I prayed but I wasn't sincere and didn't want true Deliverance. My actions revealed my unbelief that God could SAVE me. I **prayed** for strength but I wanted to fall **prey** because of the pleasure from being intimate.

When I woke the next morning, the same linen and comforter that were in my dream were the same set that I had just washed. I immediately asked God for forgiveness and bagged up everything and headed straight to the garbage can. Yes, I threw the entire set away. It represented a negative stronghold that was impeding my spiritual journey with Christ.

25

Now some of you may be wondering why I didn't just give the set away. When you deal with negative strongholds you need to destroy certain things and not pass them on to unsuspecting persons. Why would I give something to someone that I struggled with? A drug addict trying to kick drug addiction should not pass drugs on to the next person. An alcoholic should not tell drinking partners to take the liquor so they won't be tempted. A thief should not say come and get all the items I stole because I turned over a new leaf. This does not make any sense at all does it? It is not fair to hinder someone's progress with Christ.

Ref: Matthew 7:3-5

Cut off the problem at the root to ensure it does not take root and grow with anyone else.

I threw out those old dirty and filthy garments out of spiritual necessity; It was not righteous or Holy to allow someone else to adorn my dirt and filth. God stripped me down bear to show me, me. Stand before the Lord to see yourself NAKED! God will reveal what can be prayed over and given away and what should be completely discarded.

Ref: Psalm 30:10-12

Adorn the whole armor of God and never take it off. Stop playing games with the devil wearing evil, destructive clothing. Christ Jesus has new threads just for you. True repentance calls for Godly apparel. Repent and turn from evil. Do not merely ask for forgiveness. This act supplies loopholes to commit the same sin again. Only wanting forgiveness but not turning from sin is detrimental. Repent and turn from sin and do not return to that destructive place again.

Ref: Ephesians 6:10-17

The Shame

II Samuel 13:19

> **Then Tamar put ashes on her head, and tore her robe of many colors that *was* on her, and laid her hand on her head and went away crying bitterly.**

Ashes and torn garments were indications of anguish and mourning over a death. Ta'mar had become an outcast. She cried from the shame and humiliation she had just been subjected to by Am'non. Ta'mar placed ashes or dust on her head to show her deep affliction. She mourned the death of her virginity. She was untouched and pure walking in to her brother's house. She was handled and adulterated. Upon being thrown out of the same brother's house, she was contaminated and spotted. This act was a definite indication that something was wrong and would definitely draw attention to everyone who saw her. Next, Ta'mar "rent" or tore her multi-colored royal garment. If the ashes on her head were not enough surely people noticed the torn garment. Torn clothing also represented grief or anger. Lastly, Ta'mar laid her hand on her head and went on crying.

Ta'mar did not hide the fact that she was wronged. But, she also did not cry until she was out of the presence of her attacker. She did not remain outside the house of her attacker either. She moved on!

As we live our lives, there are some things and people who have taken us by force, "raped" us. So we have bent down and scooped up ashes (dust) to mark ourselves with outward projected affliction. There are issues in our lives that have caused us to tear our own garments. We need to stop hiding behind masks of perfection. We need to expose the tricks of the enemy to others to prevent the calamity from happening to someone else.

Ref: Genesis 2:7; John 20:21-23

Take a look at the list of "set ups" you have written down. Why did you act or react the way you did when certain situations arose?

Go all the way back to your childhood. Give yourself completely to God so He can purge, break, and mold you according to who you are in Him! Do not claim flaws, developed by past traumatic experiences, to become your moral compass and character. Allow the character and nature of God to transform you into a new creature.

Begin the mourning process. Deal with the shame, humiliation, and anger. Cry, shout, blow off steam. Cleanse your soul.

If at this point, you have not written the list of "set ups," stop right now and deal with the issues plaguing your life. Write them all down. God can set you free from all forms of anguish, hurt, feelings of being an outcast, and rage. I dare you to try Him!

> **They that sow in tears shall reap in joy. He that goeth forth and weepeth, bearing precious seed, shall doubtless come again with rejoicing, bringing his sheaves with him. *Psalm 126:5, 6 KJV***

The Encouragement

II Samuel 13:20, 21

> [20] **And Ab'salom her brother said to her, "Has Am'non your brother been with you? But now hold your peace, my sister. He *is* your brother; do not take this thing to heart." So Ta'mar remained desolate in her brother Ab'salom's house. [21] But when King Da'vid heard of all these things, he was very angry.**

The fifth and final contributor entered, Ab'salom, the brother of Ta'mar. Ab'salom means "My Father is Peace." A **Father** is "an originator, founder, or inventor." **Peace** is defined as "freedom from war" or "serenity or quiet." The Lord God is the Father of Peace.

Ab'salom immediately put the pieces together. He knew that Am'non did something to their sister. He knew that she entered Am'non's house untouched and, yet, there she was before him displaying signs of grief, anguish, and sorrow. Something horrible happened. The Lord knows you have gone through something unjust. Your Father also knows the times you have been unjust. God sees and feels your pain. He is waiting for you to acknowledge Him as Lord and Saviour so He can instruct you. The Holy Spirit is waiting on your will to be broken so that you may be made whole by His Will.

The Scripture does not record Ta'mar answering Ab'salom's question. He simply looked upon her countenance and instructed her to hold her peace. He told her to disregard whatever her brother Am'non did to her.

Ta'mar's grieving season was very short. The "Father is Peace" showed up, saw the hurt and bitterness, and said hold your peace. So Ta'mar remained in the house of "Peace." The Scripture declared she was desolate. **Desolate** is defined as "uninhabited." **Uninhabited** is "to have no residents." Do not think this was a bad situation. Ta'mar abided in the Father's House and lived in peace with no inhabitants of the past. In other words, Ta'mar remained in the Father of Peace baggage free.

Your Father is saying hold your peace. In other words, **hold on to your peace.** This battle is not yours but the Lord's. The weapons of your warfare are not carnal, but mighty through God. Do not relive what you have gone through. It happened and is now considered your past no matter how short the time period. You too can live without the weight of the world being on your shoulders. All those negative, self-defeating, humiliating, addictive inhabitants or residents that you are carrying around should now be served with eviction notices. It is time to kick your negative past out so that you can abide in peace.

Let's not dwell on the why's, how's, and if only King Da'vid would have done something to avenge Ta'mar. How many times have you been through something and there was no one to avenge you being victimized from some sort of injustice? Instead, focus on the fact that Ta'mar may have been bent out of shape by the violation; however, she was not broken. So should this focus be with you. Some incidents, accidents, omissions, co-missions which forced

29

you to bend did not break you. God still protected you even when you were outside of His will. However, the time has come for you to draw nearer to Him. Make up your mind. Awaken the Ta'mar Spirit within you man and woman of God. Do not be misguided. God can and will grow tired by disobedience. He will remove His covering when you refuse to return to Him. If this happens, you will never experience the Peace of God unless you repent and return unto the Father.

Ref: James 4:7-12

Conclusion

The beginning of this book is loaded with Scripture. Scriptures are the answers to all that you are going through. Scriptures are given for revealed truth in situations, instructions, encouragement, directions, and, yes even, chastisement.

Be careful about where and from whom you seek counsel concerning your spiritual walk in life. Am'non sought the wrong counsel and it cost him his very life. Jon'adab gave Am'non instructions and, yet, he went unharmed.

How many times have you encountered someone who gave you advice, only to find that they themselves did not follow their own advice? Better yet, they did not get caught up like you. Upon confrontation with these people, you find they really do not have anything to say. They might have even shrugged their shoulders as if they did not care that you stumbled upon difficulties.

If God sees all (Omnipresent), knows all (Omniscience), and has all power (Omnipotent), then why wouldn't He stop the bad things from happening? The answer: God knows that you have the Ta'mar Spirit within you. God can and will bless you with the fruit of your spiritual labor. Your experiences are now weapons that reveal the tricks of the enemy. You can fight because knowledge is gleaned. You can also help someone else fight. With God on your side, your Tests will be your Testimonies. If allowed to show and manifest His Power, God can turn EVERY situation around so that He be Magnified and Glorified.

If you read the remaining verses in II Samuel chapter 13, you will notice how Jon'adab knew that only Am'non was killed because he knew more than he let on regarding the entire situation. Everyone knows why Ab'salom killed Am'non. However, no one knew that Jon'adab encouraged Am'non to "move forward" with Ta'mar. This is how the enemy tricks us. He impels you to do things and you are chastised by your Heavenly Father. Am'non acted out of God's Will and took something very precious. Yet, he paid the ultimate price. He was murdered by his brother. Am'non was set up!

Does the enemy ever get his just reward? The answer is Yes! Romans 12:19 says, "Dearly beloved, avenge not yourselves, but rather give place unto wrath: for it is written, Vengeance is mine; I will repay, saith the Lord." In the mean time the enemy chooses the next target to trick into acting outside of God's Will. This is why it is imperative that we get in God's Word, be mouthpieces of God sharing our experiences so that others will become aware of the tricks of the enemy. A loose quote often used says, "The devil doesn't have new tricks just new people to play tricks on."

Remember, you already have the Victory by and through Jesus Christ. But, you cannot live the way you want to live and do what you want to do if it does not line up with the Word of God. You are protected as long as you stay in the ark.

Does this mean that you will not encounter trials and tribulations? No. However, you will be well equipped to deal with these trials and tribulations.

Ref: Job 14:1

Ta'mar did not compose herself or act as if nothing happened. She did not go about life all smiles and enjoying life as if she had not been violated. Neither did she become angry and take out her frustrations on people. She showed the distress. As she left

31

Am'non's house, there was no shame in letting people know that she had experienced something traumatic that day.

We have all been in denial or pretended at some point because we did not want to reveal our true state of being. We deny that our past "rapes" have affected us. Yet, we are continuously acting outside the Will of God. God said we were not of this world, yet, we indulge in worldly situations. God said we were the head and not the tail, yet, we chase after people, situations, and circumstances that do not Glorify God. God said we were above and not beneath. Yet, we hang our heads down from situational burdens. God wants us to rely on Him, yet, we attempt to HANDLE our own situations and we fail. We state that God has all power but our actions reveal that we don't truly believe God is Omnipotent.

By and through the Mighty Awesome Omnipotent Power of God virginity can be obtained again. Purity and wholeness can be restored. Seek and acknowledge God. Trust He is able to do exceedingly and abundantly above and beyond what finite minds can think. Pray and fast. Yes, FAST! If Jesus told the disciples that these things come by prayer and fasting when it comes to certain evil spirits, then yes, beloved you have to pray and FAST.

Ref: Mark 9:28-29

Surround yourself with positive people who are within the body of Christ that are mature in Christ. Just because someone is a positive and kind hearted person doesn't mean they are good for you, if they are not saved. All their goodness and acts of kindness are for naught. Unbelievers do not believe Jesus is their Lord and Saviour. Believers profess Christ.

A believer trusts the Bible because God manifested Himself as the written Word. A person must not straddle the fence of agnosticism. Believers are lights that show the un-church that Jesus is alive and lives in us through the Holy Spirit. The lights of the true temples of God are bright billboards announcing, advertising, declaring, and persuading the unsaved people of the world that

God can save, set free, heal, and deliver. Worshippers and Praisers become living testimonies for God.

Concerning matters of the soul, it is dangerous to commit to being good, practicing random acts of kindness, as well as claiming piety minus Jesus Christ. Non-committal to attending church, studying the Word of God, and continuing in worldly immoderations are damaging to the divine nature of man.

It is imperative to have a relationship with the Father. Having the lingo will not produce Holy spiritual fruit. **Relationship** means a "connection by blood or marriage." Christ's blood redeems and connects us to Him. To **Connect** means "to join or to show or think of as related." A connection is made and relationship develops through Jesus' death, burial, and resurrection. God can come into every person's heart and establish a relationship with Him. With relationship comes the Truth of God. The Truth of God inspired by the Holy Spirit will lead every person to the right path that is lighted by Christ.

Ref: Romans 1:21-25

Place yourself around mighty men and women of God, who are in right relationship with God, to minister to you and encourage you on this spiritual journey. These men and women should live a Holy lifestyle that is pleasing unto God. Be able to take correction in order to grow. Do not pray and ask God to move on your behalf if you are not willing to allow Him to move in His timing. It is time to stop playing and get real with where we are in God and where God wants us to be in Him. The Lord is getting ready to snatch the covers off of hidden, secret postures that do not line up with His Word.

Ref: Hebrews 10:16-23; James 1:1-8

There is something about having a calling on your life. You cannot act, say, nor do what others do when you are the called of God. You find yourself struggling more than those in the world. You may or may not have completely surrendered to God. But, you find that you experience trials and tribulations and are compelled to take matters to God. God has chosen you. Like it or not, God thinks you are worthy to have spiritual burdens placed on you. He said in His Word that He would place no more on you than you could bear. God knows that you have been shouldering burdens and He now desires to release the Ta'mar Spirit within you.

Record of "Set-ups"

Chapter 3

Where Are You?

And they heard the voice of the LORD God walking in the garden in the cool of the day: and Adam and his wife hid themselves from the presence of the LORD God amongst the trees of the garden. And the LORD God called unto Adam, and said unto him, Where art thou? Genesis 3:8, 9 KJV

Like most people, I had numerous situations where the enemy repeatedly tried to destroy me; situations like being threatened with a gun, participating in illegal activities, being spat on, and being taken advantage of. I've loaned money to people who never repaid me, experimented with drugs, drank alcohol, and even battled severe depression while suicidal. The list went on and on. Each one of these trying situations had me bent out of shape, but I was not broken. I searched deep within myself and got to the root of why I behaved and tolerated certain things as well as certain people in my life. I desired to have peace in my life. I was tired of the turmoil. So I surrounded myself with bold Soldiers in Christ. I did not yet possess the peace I was seeking but I knew they possessed what I needed. The saints of God nurtured me and I am blessed to have the peace I knew He desired me to discover and have.

We have sometimes experienced the same tests of life over and over again never seeming to pass them. It is time to stop taking repeat tests. Are you ready? I declare that this book will start you on your way to freedom and finally passing these tests. It has been a continuous journey and I am still learning and growing in God. While on this journey, it is my sincerest desire to help you go through the tests of life you are facing.

Follow me as I continue to follow Christ on this journey to reveal the Ta'mar Spirit in you. What is the Ta'mar Spirit? The Ta'mar Spirit is being able to dwell in the House of the Father of Peace and living uninhabited by negative, past experiences. It is the Spirit of Peace. God's Spirit is one of peace and as you take on more characteristics of the Father, the Lord's peace will grow within you.

Ta'mar was the daughter of King Da'vid like we are the sons and daughters of the King of Kings, Jesus Christ. We are to bear our Cross because we are connected and are part of the Divine lineage. Our lives have consisted of journeys of ups and downs, of achievements and disappointments, of advances and setbacks.

We all have been through some major life altering encounters. Some people know how to seek God for release and are delivered; while other people do not know how to seek Him. We all should become aware that God is our protector and burden bearer. No matter where a person is in life, there comes a time where the Delivering Power of Jesus is needed. The situation has to be dealt with head on. It is time to stop sweeping dirty little secrets under the carpet. Stop hiding skeletons in the closet. At some point in life, a reality check is necessary for advancement and growth in the Kingdom of God. Ask the tough questions. WHAT am I really doing in my walk with Christ? WHY can't I seem to get past THIS situation? HOW do I make it through this obstacle PERMANENTLY? Am I truly walking according to God's divine purpose for my life? These questions need to be asked and then answered no matter how startling the truth may be. Let's begin the journey to discover, uncover, destroy, and recover. It is time to deal with the inner spirit man so that peace may abound in your life. Ready?

Let's pray…

> *Father God in the name of Jesus Christ, I come to You Lord in a meek and humble way. Lord I ask right now that You purge me. Holy Spirit, empty out all forms of mannerisms, isms, and schisms that are not in Your Precious Will for me God. Lord I come before You God. Lord I submit to the fact that You have ALL power. Lord I know that because You have ALL power, I am now ready to turn my life, my heart, my mind, my soul, my EVERYTHING over to You right now. Lord I leave myself exposed to You. Lord I ask that You cover me with Your Wonderful and Marvelous LOVE. I pray this*

prayer in Faith and I claim the Victory in Your name Jesus. Amen.

Before proceeding, read: II Samuel Chapters 11 & 12…

…Welcome back!

Now here's the first reality check question. Did you actually stop to read those two chapters entirely or did you simply continue reading?

If you read the chapters great! It shows that you are a step further in obtaining the Ta'mar Spirit. You know when to grab your weapon (The Holy Bible). The enemy cannot be defeated and the soul cannot be enlightened if the Word of God is never wielded properly.

If you did not stop to pick up your weapon (The Holy Bible), then your first lesson is to ALWAYS read your Bible when delving in any mind altering, soul changing journey. You need to be fed the right nourishment. Nevertheless, picking up the Word of God and reading it RIGHT NOW makes for a mighty weapon to wield.

> **Study to shew thyself approved unto God, a workman that needeth not to be ashamed, rightly dividing the word of truth. *II Timothy 2:15 KJV***

Now, if you happen to fall into the earlier "I did not stop and read" category, the question still remains, did you stop and read?

If you did, then great! It shows that you are now one step closer to identifying with the Ta'mar Spirit.

If you still did not read, there is a spiritual blockage preventing you from utilizing the Word of God as a weapon to defeat the enemy.

Let's pray…

> **Father God in the name of Jesus, I need Your help Lord. Forgive me Jesus for not turning to Your Word. Lord I sometimes feel overwhelmed and lost when I read.**

Father at other times, I am not motivated to read Your Word. Lord I ask that You make Your Word digestible. Lord, I rebuke all the symptoms of confusion and frustration I have felt in the past. I come against the lazy spirit in the name of Jesus. Father I turn to You and I declare and decree that I can read Your Word with clarity, understanding, and ease. Jesus I know that You are not the author of confusion. Therefore, I bind all manner of demonic blockage over my life. Lord God I loose by the authority and power of Jesus Christ new revelations of Your Word. Lord I thank You for revealing Yourself to me through Your Holy Spirit and Your Word. Continue to rid me of any form of laziness, confusion, frustration, or anything that prevents me from going deeper in You Lord. In Jesus' name I declare I have the victory. In Jesus' name I decree excitement and joy in Your Word. Amen.

You are very precious and you deserve to know the truth. Always remember that in order for things to work out, you must follow Christ through His Word in Spirit and in Truth.

You are not on this journey alone. It does not matter if you fell into the first, second, or even third group. You still have the victory by and through Jesus Christ! Simply begin to study to show yourself approved unto God. This is the only way to rightly divide the Word of Truth.

So what is happening when it appears that God does not hear your cry? There are three possible answers which come to mind. First, God has already provided instructions for you that you do not like so you continue praying, hoping for a different answer. An answer that you want God to bless you with because you really do not want to do what was instructed. If you fall into this first category, repent for ignoring the instructions of the Lord and do what He has told you to do.

Seek ye the LORD while he may be found, call ye upon him while he is near: Let the wicked forsake his way, and the unrighteous man his thoughts: and let him return unto the LORD, and he will have mercy upon him; and to our God, for he will abundantly pardon. For my thoughts are not your thoughts, neither are your ways my ways, saith the LORD. For as the heavens are higher than the earth, so are my ways higher than your ways, and my thoughts than your thoughts. For as the rain cometh down, and the snow from heaven, and returneth not thither, but watereth the earth, and maketh it bring forth and bud, that it may give seed to the sower, and bread to the eater: So shall my word be that goeth forth out of my mouth: it shall not return unto me void, but it shall accomplish that which I please, and it shall prosper in the thing whereto I sent it. For ye shall go out with joy, and be led forth with peace. *Isaiah 55:6-12a KJV*

The second possible answer is that maybe a person has not accepted the Lord Jesus Christ *in* their lives.

Therefore now amend your ways and your doings, and obey the voice of the LORD your God; and the LORD will repent him of the evil that he hath pronounced against you. *Jeremiah 26:13 KJV*

Now we know that God heareth not sinners: but if any man be a worshiper of God, and doeth his will, him he heareth. *John 9:31 KJV*

Repent ye therefore, and be converted, that your sins may be blotted out, when the times of refreshing shall come from the presence of the Lord. *Acts 3:19 KJV*

If you fall into this second category you must be saved. How do you get saved? Simply do this...

That if thou shalt confess with thy mouth the Lord Jesus, and shalt believe in thine heart that God hath raised him from the dead, thou shalt be saved. For with the heart man believeth unto righteousness; and with the mouth confession is made unto salvation. *Romans 10:9, 10 KJV*

And when he had called the people unto him with his disciples also, he said unto them, Whosoever will come after me, let him deny himself, and take up his cross, and follow me. For whosoever will save his life shall lose it; but whosoever shall lose his life for my sake and the gospel's, the same shall save it. For what shall it profit a man, if he shall gain the whole world, and lose his own soul? Or what shall a man give in exchange for his soul? Whosoever therefore shall be ashamed of me and of my words in this adulterous and sinful generation; of him also shall the Son of man be ashamed, when he cometh in the glory of his Father with the holy angels. *Mark 8:34-38 KJV*

The final possible answer is that God has already answered and is moving on your behalf although you do not see the manifestation of your answered prayers. If you fall into this last category, WAIT.

Wait on the LORD: be of good courage, and he shall strengthen thine heart: wait, I say, on the LORD. *Psalm 27:14 KJV*

Our soul waiteth for the LORD: he is our help and our shield. *Psalm 33:20 KJV*

Rest in the LORD, and wait patiently for him: fret not thyself because of him who prospereth in his way, because of the man who bringeth wicked devices to pass. *Psalm 37:7 KJV*

Additional Scriptures to research: Romans 3:23, Isaiah 53:6, Acts 16:30, 31, John 3:26, Luke 13:3, Isaiah 55:7, John 3:16, Revelation 3:20, and I John 5:12.

There was a woman with an issue of blood who had a great burden she was bearing. She went from physician to physician and could not obtain favorable results. The more she sought relief the sicker she got. She spent all of her money pursuing healing. Yet, she never gave up. She had been battling in her own strength for twelve long years. She was growing tired and desperation set in. There was a growing buzz about a man named Jesus. The crowd was gathering because Jesus was coming. The one who was healing was getting ready to pass by her way. What did this woman do? She turned her desperation into determination. She was going to be healed this day. Although the crowd was great she did not let that stop her. She decided that she could be made whole by just touching the hem of Jesus' garment. So she crouched down to get in position.

It is interesting that this position also established humility. The Word of God says that when a person is weak, He is made strong. She didn't exalt herself and demand healing. She humbled herself and got down before the Master Physician. Here He comes. She is ready! She reaches out. She makes contact with His hem. Wait! Something is happening... "I am whole! The blood has been dried." The woman's determination had just turned into deliverance. Yet, she stays hidden. She doesn't announce to the crowd that she was just immediately made whole.

Then it happens. Jesus stops and asks, "Who touched me?" But she had only touched his garment; the hem of His garment at that. There is no way He could have felt her touch. When you reach out to touch Christ, no matter how big the crowd the Lord will always feel His children's touch. He begins to scan the crowd. His disciples are trying to convince Him that the crowd is too great to seek out one single person. Jesus ignores them and the woman realizes she has been found out. She rises from her position, steps forward to own up to what she did, and bows at His feet. She tells Him that she was the one who touched Him. Jesus responds, "thy faith hath made thee whole; **go in peace**, and be whole of thy plague." The woman's faith attracted Jesus' attention. No matter where she went, He wanted her to go in peace. He also wanted her to be whole because she had just connected with Him.

Connecting with Jesus will produce positive changes in your life; eliminating all plagues. Even if you are like the man who was crippled with palsy, your sins can be forgiven. The man's friends broke the roof of the house in order to bring the man closer to Jesus. They lowered him down from the rooftop and because of their faith; the man's sins were forgiven. There are always saints of God praying on your behalf; breaking the roof off of your situations to lower you to the feet of Jesus. These people are called intercessors; they pray to God and the Holy Spirit leads them to pray for people they may or may not know. Prayer warriors are only concerned about praying for souls. They do not have to know the person and the situation because God sees and knows the whole of the matter.

You connect to Jesus by faith. Faith is believing against the reality of the situation. Faith is realizing that you are part of something and someone bigger than yourself. Faith receives the unseen promises and blessings of Christ Jesus. Out of faith births peace.

Everyone desires peace. Whether saved or not, living righteous or not, everyone is pursuing peace. Worldly peace is temporal. Kingdom peace is everlasting.

Becoming part of the Kingdom of God yields eternal rewards. It doesn't matter what is plaguing you. You cannot be healed in your own strength. But God can heal you. Forget about the busy bodies who are always gossiping and tearing people down with their words. God will exalt you even before your enemies' eyes. It doesn't matter how you look physically because that is just a trick of the enemy. The Lord wants you to come as you are so that you may be covered in the ark of safety. It doesn't matter if you have an addiction. The Holy Spirit will purge you completely. If you are enduring abuse, come out. There are REAL saints who have been trained to lead you out through Jesus Christ. He is the gate in which all sheep enter in. Allow the Holy Spirit to shepherd you into the fold. He loves you so much that He is looking for you. God wants to bring you back home. He wants you out of harm's way. Can you hear Him calling? "Where art thou?"

Remember the list of "set ups" you were writing down? This list should now be discarded. Throw them away! Burn them if you desire. Get rid of all of those nagging reminders that keep you from serving God fully. These issues will no longer lead you to believe you are not worthy to be considered an heir in the Kingdom of God. You are worthy! Dwell in the house of the Father. He is your Peace.

Father God in the name of Jesus, I am ready to receive. Lord I ask that You rid me of all negativity I have been holding onto. Lord I ask that You teach me to release the pain that I may no longer relive past hurts. Lord move me forward into Your precious purpose, plan, and will for my life. I thank You Father and call it done in the name of Jesus. Thank You Lord for healing my heart, mind, and soul. Thank You for purging me and shedding Your blood to cleanse me. Continue working on me Lord as I continue to yield and submit to You Holy Spirit. Amen

Chapter 4

What is a Testimony?

To this John replied, "A man can receive only what is given him from heaven. You yourselves can testify that I said, 'I am not the Christ but am sent ahead of him.' The bride belongs to the bridegroom. The friend who attends the bridegroom waits and listens for him, and is full of joy when he hears the bridegroom's voice. That joy is mine, and it is now complete. **He must become greater; I must become less.** *"The one who comes from above is above all; the one who is from the earth belongs to the earth, and speaks as one from the earth. The one who comes from heaven is above all. He testifies to what he has seen and heard, but no one accepts his testimony.* **The man who has accepted it has certified that God is truthful.** *For the one whom God has sent speaks the words of God, for God gives the Spirit without limit. The Father loves the Son and has placed everything in his hands. Whoever believes in the Son has eternal life, but whoever rejects the Son will not see life, for God's wrath remains on them. John 3:27-36 NIV*

An unknown author penned this phrase: "The Old Testament is the New Testament Concealed. The New Testament is the Old Testament Revealed." In other words, God created and established and ordained every single second that ticks into a new present. Therefore, God knew that in forty-two generations Jesus would be born. Knowing this, God gave clues to the Old Testament saints that a Saviour was coming. When God created the first Adam, rules were established. The only requirement was obedience to God's Word and Adam and Eve could subdue and have dominion over ALL of God's creation. They were in direct fellowship and relationship with God until sin entered by way of disobedience. The relationship was broken and sacrifices were required upon exile from Eden. These sacrifices were needed on a continual basis until Jesus Christ, the second Adam, would arrive. Our Saviour would be the ultimate sacrifice to remove sin and redeem those who believed. It only took Jesus to be a onetime sacrifice to restore the broken relationship with the Father. Through Christ our fellowship is now recovered. Jesus Christ was spoken of in the Old Testament but He had yet to arrive. Consequently, when Jesus arrived all of the prophecies from the Old Testament prophets began to come to pass. The Old Testament mysteries were being revealed.

Why is this Old Testament, New Testament axiom imperative; because we must bear witness of the goodness of Jesus Christ who we profess to be the head of our lives. We must tell people of the hurdles we have had to jump over, the valleys we have had to walk through, the peaks we have had to climb up, and the rivers we have had to wade across.

We are bombarded with complex scenarios that we must navigate over, under, around, and through. We get discouraged, ashamed, bitter, angry, sad but God still requires us to press towards the mark of a higher calling which is in Christ Jesus. In order to strengthen one another we must share testimonies of how God stepped in and made a way out of no way. We must be witnesses that God is real and still answers prayers. Our testimonies are important because people who MAY NOT understand the Bible WILL understand someone who has personally experienced a move of God. A testimony allows people to catch hold of the declaration that we serve a true and living God.

What is a testimony? A **Testimony** is a, "statement made under oath to establish a fact; any declaration; or any form of evidence, proof." Everyone understands the fact of people making announcements about the subject or hot topic of the hour. The world media systems have created multifaceted avenues in which to make statements and voice opinions. It does not matter whether these declarations line up according to the Word of God because the world does not recognize God. However, we as bondservants of Christ must begin making oaths and presenting proof that God can save a wretched sinner because He saved you and He saved me. We must begin to give our testimony in such a way that there is no room for doubting that God exists.

Spiritually speaking, how is the word testimony termed? **Testimony** in the Old Testament is **Edut** which refers to, "ordinances or the Ten Commandments. It deals with solemn divine charges or duties." The Ten Commandments were known and are referred to as "the testimony."

As we look at the New Testament, **Testimony** is characterized as **Marturion** which "takes on subjection of a person's personal experience; a witness who focuses on Christ and points people to Christ."

Both Testament and Testimony contain the word test. **Test** is secularly explained as, "an event that tries one's qualities; a set of questions, for determining one's knowledge, or a trial or reaction for identifying a substance." What are you made of? When life presses hard up against you and has you in a vice grip will the Holy Spirit be the substance which oozes out?

In the Spiritual, **Test** is **Tsarap**, which means, "to refine, try, and smelt." **Testing** came to be known as, "refining by means of suffering." When you call on the name of the Lord you become a purified, covenant keeper. The Word of God alone has been tried over the span of time and has been found as a true purifier. **Test** is an action word. Knowing that it is an action word or some type of movement or exerted energy makes it clear that a **Testimony** is "the quintessential forward progression of catapulting God's Word to a dark world." We must become shining lights and give our "Test"imony of how we went through the fire but came out unscathed yet purified.

We have all been through or are in the midst of some type of struggle. We have all witnessed some type of tragedy that influenced us in some fashion. We have all made decisions to do or not to do certain things. We have all been in dry and desolate places.

The question then becomes, if you are still in a dry place in your life, do you want to be set free? God is a God who can do the impossible. Your current situation is nothing for God. Do you want to be made whole? I pray your answer to both questions is Yes!

47

Father God in the matchless name of Jesus Christ, I come to You asking forgiveness of sin I committed against You God. Lord, I have failed to trust in Your Holy Word. Lord, I have doubted that You could deliver me at times. Lord, I have even sometimes questioned Your Omniscient wisdom. Lord, I come now with my head hung down in a posture of humbleness. Lord, I come before You. Lord, I yield and submit to You. Lord God, I declare You are my Master Physician. Operate on me Lord! Remove all matters that are not of You Jesus. Lord, help me hear and receive how others have given their testimonies in order for me to realize that You can Deliver me as well. God, I cannot do anything without You and I am tired of trying. Lord Jesus, I cry out to You. Help Lord! Save me Lord! Heal me Lord! Deliver me Lord! I pour out unto You God everything that I have been trying to battle in my own strength. I give these issues over to You Jesus. I make a solemn vow to never pick these issues, situations, and circumstances back up again. Lord, I make a transition of thanksgiving in my prayer to You. Lord, thank You for being a burden bearer. Jesus, I thank You for making a way out of no way. Lord God, thank You for being the Master Judge, Jury, and Counselor. I thank You Jesus for having the final Word in my life. Thank You for tearing me down and building me back up God according to Your Divine Purpose and Holy Plan. I submit unto Your Will for my life Lord. Thank You Holy Spirit for rising up in me and leading me in Holy, Divine Truth. Amen.

Here are some simple words to remember: **You can make it with God.** Jesus hung, bled, died, and rose that we might live. No matter what you have gone through or are currently going through just know that you can make it with God. You are a living testimony. Whether you are a believer of Christ or not, everyone has a testimony. What makes the testimony powerful is the Spirit of God. Testimony brought forth of deliverance and triumph backed by the power of God establishes a power greater than self. In self there may be power but it is not miraculous power. In self there is temporary strength but no joy because the joy of the Lord is strength. God's super attached to your natural makes you supernatural.

Ref: Revelation 2:1-7

You may be hurting from the fiery darts being launched at you, but God wants you to trust Him and remain in Peace. Your health may be faulty. Your appetite for unhealthy fixations may be causing you to become weaker. Your lifestyle and finances may seem to be lacking. Whatever the current state of your condition may be, just know God desires that you remain in Peace. When you have His Peace, it will truly surpass all understanding. Allow God's Peace to permeate your entire being. Allow God's very presence by way of the Holy Spirit to saturate every area of your life. I promise your life will experience a transformation. People will see God working in your life. They will begin to take notice of the marvelous Light that is inundating you. They will be forced to see the Holy Spirit resting in you and upon you. People will be in awe of how you are able to cope with situations in the midst of a storm. People will grow in curiosity as to how you are surviving. They will become dumbfounded by the mere fact you are still alive.

I read these words, "Certificate of Registration," when I looked up from typing. This certificate was issued to me pursuant to a specific state Statute. What does a Certificate of Registration grant? It bestows me rights to operate within the State. It does not matter whether I conduct business or not, I have the authority to do so. In Christ Jesus, by His death, burial, and resurrection, we were given certificates that registered us with the Kingdom. This is, of course, for those who are born again but still struggling.

If you have not been saved, there is still a certificate of registration waiting for you. Repent and be baptized for the pardoning of your sins. Believe that Jesus Christ died on your behalf. Once you do, the certificate of registration is issued. Jesus Christ already paid the price.

You have the authority to operate in the Kingdom. While operating you have to advertise. Advertising attracts business. You gain customers. Christ said that if He be lifted up from the earth He would draw all men unto Him. This is what your testimony does. It attracts people. They want to know more about your business; your business of shedding light on a grim situation. People want to know how they can get this special light that destroys darkness. Guess what? Your testimony allows you to operate by and through the certificate of registration.

God through His statutes empowers you to function in His Kingdom. As I peered over my laptop at the certificate, I read the bottom line: has met registration requirements for the business location stated above and is authorized…This certificate is non-transferable. POST THIS CERTIFICATE IN A CONSPICUOUS PLACE. When God created you He knew every supply you would need to prosper you in this life. Once you have this certificate, you cannot transfer it to someone else. You do not even have to worry about someone attempting to steal your certificate because there is a specific number assigned to you as well. God's Word says He knows the plans He has for you. Therefore, He has exacted certain circumstances to cause you to acquire explicit skill sets and talents. Who better to be instrumental in the deliverance of a drug addict than someone delivered from drugs? Who better to be influential in the deliverance of a foolish person than a person who has made foolish mistakes? God has given us all unique certifications through the powerful resurrection of Jesus Christ and the blood and water shed on the Cross. Do not be afraid of the authority vested in you by the King. God's statutes which are laid out in the Holy Bible are the law. Give your testimony once God brings you out. Better yet, give a testimony of praise while you are still going through. God is worthy of the praise before, during, and after the storm. Glorify Him and watch Him move on your behalf. You are His exquisite creation.

You were made, hand crafted even in the image of God. God is incorruptible. He is a strong tower that does not shift nor sway. He took His time forming you. He thought about you. He imagined you in the Spirit of His mind. He created your present, past, and future. He knew the precise moments when you would get into trouble and created angels to be there at exact moments to help you. He knew the moments when you would slip, trip, and fall. Yet, He took His time and created you. Why; because you were put together by the Master Carpenter who can make no mistakes. What He makes is indestructible. He knew that you would be able to last during the storm. He knew you would get dirty in the storm as well. He knew you would sometimes not bathe in His Glory and the dirt would continue to pile up from the next storm. But God knew that you would endure. God also knew when you would earnestly seize the Revelation for your life. God knew the exact moment that you would surrender everything over to Him.

Grab hold of the Spiritual Truth in God's Word. God wants to use you. He wants you to share your testimony with someone so they too can be delivered and set free.

Ref: Ecclesiastes 11:1-6

It is not for us to know ALL things. If we did I believe we would go crazy. Think about your life and where God brought you from. If He showed you ALL the hell you would have to go through in order to get your breakthrough you would probably give in and give out before the storm even formed. God knows how much we can bear and He safeguards us through the Holy Spirit, our Comforter. God requires love and obedience from us. These are simple requirements, yet, we sometimes feel these are too complex for us to handle. The love we have familiarity with is perverted. We have a distorted sense of what to expect from the love we receive. When God extends His loving arms we reject His advance because His love gives the impression of being an imposter. We have been fooled for so long that the very thing we define as love is the REAL imposter. Yet, God continues to reach for us, ready to embrace us as soon as we allow Him to touch us in that secret intimate way.

Ref: Proverbs 8:32-36

There is a war going on, on your behalf. Heavenly angels assigned to you are fighting demonic angels. God loves you so much that He will wage war on your behalf. He is dispatching warring angels who are warriors. These angels fight to win! God counted up the cost and decided you were worth the war. You will be blessed by the proceeding chapter of testimonies. Come into the revelation of your worth in God. This Godly, revelational knowledge is a gradual progression. The advancement of knowledge gives birth to victories won. You can and will be victorious. Keep pursuing

God. Keep fighting to stay connected to the Lord God Almighty. You can do it with the Spirit of God. He will encourage you. He will lift you up. He will give you a place of refuge in Him.

Life and death are in the power of the tongue. The choice is yours to speak life. A testimony will speak life to those who have cursed themselves to die with their thoughts, speech, actions, and inactions. The ultimate testimony is that of Jesus Christ. The Living Word tells how He endured persecution. Yet, He overcame and ascended into Heaven to take His rightful seat beside the Father. Testimonies are wonderful because God is Glorified. Testimonies strengthen the measure of faith given to every believer. The Word of God confirms that we are more than conquerors through Christ Jesus. The reason being is that we have applied the Word of God to our lives. Faithful testimonies tell of the faithfulness of God.

The first use of testimony came in Exodus. **Exodus** means "to depart or go out." The children of Is'rael were on the verge of coming out of bondage. God gave Moses instructions to lay up items before the Lord to be kept for all generations to remember. An ark was precisely and concisely prepared. The ark represents you. The Lord instructed that His commands, precepts, and so on be placed inside. As you become an ark for God, the same is expected of you. Become a living testimony because you carry the Word within. If it had not been for the Lord and Godly favor you would not be where you are at this moment. The storm may be raging; however, you are alive to experience it.

Jesus is the ultimate ark example. All within Him was His Fathers instructions. The miracles, signs and wonders that went forth were because of what was on the inside of Him. Jesus Christ did nothing in the flesh. Even when betrayed by Judas and it would appear that the ark of Jesus the Messiah would fail it did not. The ark prevailed. The testimony went forth that Jesus the Christ rose with all power. If you believe the Bible to be the TRUTH, the living Word of God, then you believe the testimonies within it. If Jesus overcame then so can you. The enemy and his instruments are defeated. You have to just start living a victorious life proclaiming the gospel and giving testimony as examples of victories won through Christ.

The pages of life are very intriguing. They contain the language of Best Sellers. From suspense, to thrillers, to danger, to comedy, and so on our lives have had no match on any non-fiction book on the shelf of bookstores today. The next chapter will present five testimonies from people who exhibit the Ta'mar Spirit. These are modern day examples of people who have had trials and tribulations in their life. They have had serious bouts with the enemy. They were bent but God held them up. They strayed from His presence but God drew them near again. Are you in need of a "But God" in this season of your life? Surrender to the One who can pull the possible out of the impossible. Awaken the Ta'mar Spirit within you.

Chapter 5

Living Testimonies

*And there was war in heaven: Michael and his angels fought against the dragon; and the dragon fought and his angels, And prevailed not; neither was their place found any more in heaven. And the great dragon was cast out, that old serpent, called the Devil, and Satan, which deceiveth the whole world: he was cast out into the earth, and his angels were cast out with him. And I heard a loud voice saying in heaven, Now is come salvation, and strength, and the kingdom of our God, and the power of his Christ: for the accuser of our brethren is cast down, which accused them before our God day and night. **And they overcame him by the blood of the Lamb, and by the word of their testimony; and they loved not their lives unto the death.** Revelation 12:7-11 KJV*

This chapter connects you with five different testimonies. You may connect with one or all of them. They made it with God. These soldiers in the Lord possess the Ta'mar Spirit; the ability to go through the storm. They have experienced the gale winds, torrential rains, and flying debris from obstacles and yet they were not destroyed. You have the Ta'mar Spirit in you as well. These testimonies have been divinely chosen by God. God wants you to abide in peace without destructive, negative inhabitants. People looking from the outside may count you out based on the fleshly appearance. But GOD...

The Holy Spirit led me to Believers who have powerful testimonies and they always return any semblance of praise back to the Lord; Mountain movers who are not afraid to give God Glory. These Peculiar people are not ashamed to share their testimony so that others may witness God working in their lives. These ambassadors of God have experienced the storms of life. They have sometimes strayed away from God but they have always returned to Him. God is their first LOVE. Because they have experienced real love in and of God, they allow peace to follow them. They walk peaceably. The storms of life are transformed by speaking the Word...Peace be still.

It does not matter how many times you mess up and fall. What matters is that you return to God. Realize that He is your first LOVE. You are His ark. He has placed Himself in you by way of the Holy Spirit. Do not be ashamed of the testimony within you.

GOD'S MIRACLE

O taste and see that the LORD is good: blessed is the man that trusteth in him. *Psalm 34:8 KJV*

In 2004, my spouse and I decided we were ready to have a child. In our attempts to conceive, nothing happened. Satan was blocking our blessing. It was truly a spiritual attack because the doctor could not detect physiological issues.

We tried for the next year to year and a half with the same results. We both began to pray and I sought the saints of God for the laying on of hands in 2005. An ultrasound revealed something startling - Tumors! The doctor stated that this was the cause of us not conceiving. He was trying to abort what was promised us by God. But GOD...

Again believing and taking God at His word; the Body of Christ **stood**, **touched**, and **agreed** that we would conceive. Giving God all the Glory and Honor which is due unto Him, we became pregnant in 2005. Our son was born on July 28, 2006. As he grows, the anointing grows on his life; to God be the Glory.

Ref: Deuteronomy 28:1-14

BATTLES FOUGHT, VICTORIES WON

Have mercy upon me, O God, according to thy lovingkindness: according unto the multitude of thy tender mercies blot out my transgressions. Wash me throughly from mine iniquity, and cleanse me from my

sin. **For I acknowledge my transgressions: and my sin is
ever before me.** *Psalm 51:1-3 KJV*

While sitting pondering life and ALL God has seen them through,
these words of reflection were penned.

I can remember like it was yesterday when the doctor said it was
cancer. Evidence had been building that something was wrong for
one whole year. But I would not think about it. I went on ignoring
all symptoms for another year or so. When I finally went to a
doctor, surgery and medicine were the only choices given me. But,
I knew Jesus to be a Healer and I said, "Do what you want because
it is in God's Hand and by His stripes I am healed." I started
hearing all kinds of things such as cancer is so very bad. It can kill
you. This thing (your issue) is bad. To make matters more
unnerving, I did not have any insurance at that time.

Having heard all of these negative words being spoken, I reached
for my Bible. I started reading Psalm 91.

Ref: Psalm 91:1-16

I stood on God's Word and said, "By Jesus' stripes I AM healed!"
I had surgery and the doctors were able to remove all cancerous
cells. I knew everything was over. I recovered really well all while
thanking God even in my follow-up doctor's visits. The doctor
told me because there was nothing to treat (there was no cancer
left) there was no need for any sort of treatment
(chemotherapy/radiation).

One year later, my body was attacked by cancer again. I was tired
of this battle! But GOD in His infinite wisdom blessed me to have
insurance. With insurance came doctor referrals. Before, the
doctor simply suggested having surgery. I had another subsequent
operation followed by chemotherapy treatments. This was the
hardest time of my life. The medicine made me sick and my entire
body was racked with pain. All I could do was pray and remember
God's words, "No matter what you go through, I will be with you."
I felt like Jesus in the Garden of Gethsemane; God let this cup pass
on by me. However, I knew God wanted me well. So I pressed

my way and persevered. Well, my insurance lapsed just before I received my last chemotherapy treatment. I called the doctor and said, "I do not have insurance anymore." God granted me favor because the doctor's response was for me to come on anyway to get the treatment. He said not to worry about the bill. After some convincing by my spouse, I returned to the doctor. I was extremely tired of being sick from the medication and had grown weary in my well doing. I thank God I am alive and well today. God took care of me in spite of me.

FAITH THROUGH THE FIRE
"I've Been Through the Fire, But I Don't Smell Like Smoke"

Behold, I will do a new thing; now it shall spring forth; shall ye not know it? I will even make a way in the wilderness, and rivers in the desert. *Isaiah 43:19 KJV*

Everything about the odds in my life said that I should not be where I am today. In fact, most people who had endured what I lived through would have probably thrown in the towel. But GOD...

God is so faithful and just to deliver us from all kinds of problems and dilemmas. In spite of our many weaknesses, God shows Himself strong and mighty. I am honored to say that these words have proven true in my life over and over again.

A product of a single-parent home, I was raised by a woman who was already old enough to be my grandmother when I was born, the pressure of which caused her to suffer from a nervous breakdown. Following her subsequent diagnosis with paranoid schizophrenia, I spent several years coping with her mental health issues that miraculously subsided after I turned sixteen. The youngest of three children (my brother and I are seventeen years apart and my sister and I are fifteen years apart), my mom sent me to college on a salary of $5,000 a year and oftentimes both of us went without in order to keep me in school. After four long years, I was able to finally finish school and have my 68-year-old mother by my side.

58

Following my graduation from Florida A&M University in 1988 with a Bachelor in Science degree in Journalism, I began a reporting job at the local newspaper company in May 1988.

Months later, I married and began a new and challenging life as a spouse and parent. The combination of the two, followed by two near-death surgical experiences, and a very limited joint salary, were extremely difficult. In fact, we faced foreclosure numerous times. At one point, during our young marriage, we had no more than a few dollars left after paying all of our bills. I had finally met poverty – face to face. I did not have money for basics, such as food and clothes. Because my finances were so bad, I was not even able to make enough money to pay my car note, which I eventually decided to return to the bank before they could repossess it. For a period, I had to drive less than perfect cars from buy-here, pay-here lots that rarely lasted more than a few months. Credit card bills and other debts mounted as the money was not enough to cover the expenses. Needless to say, the financial deficit put a terrible strain on the marriage and we, on numerous occasions, contemplated divorce.

At this point, although I was a believer and knew God was a Deliverer, I believed Satan when he convinced me that I was not worthy of God's blessings. I believed Satan when he said "If God loved you, He would not let you suffer." My doubt and lack of faith opened the door to Satan's devices and schemes. And at one of the lowest points in my life – pending foreclosure, loss of a job and a car – I made one of the biggest mistakes of my life – a mistake that cost me a trip to jail, ten years probation and thousands of dollars in court costs, fines, and penalties.

How would I ever bounce back from this? Why didn't God help me? And why didn't I realize that God was testing me to see if I would continue to trust Him in the bad times, just as I had in the good times? It was then that I decided to repent and turn back to God and trust Him again.

Once I realized that God truly loved and cared about me and would supply all of my needs according to His riches in Glory, I began to watch God turn things around drastically in my life. It was when I was at my WORST, that God saw my WORTH.

With His help and through total submission and reliance on Him, He rescued me and began to restore all that the cankerworm had eaten. Despite the SETBACK, God had SET ME UP to be blessed beyond measure. With a new job, an increased salary, a new car and a newborn baby, I went back to FAMU in 1997 and obtained a Master of Education Degree in Mental Health Counseling. Following that, I was accepted as a doctoral candidate in the Ph. D. program. All of that prepared me to work for the State of Florida for twenty years, while serving as a FAMU professor in the School of Journalism and Graphic Arts, where I taught Mass Media Methods for six years. To coin the words of singer/songwriter Apostle Rosilyn Copeland, "It took all of that, to get to this."

Indeed the odds were against me, but God made the difference. And when I look back over my life, I realize that I have a reason to thank God for His grace and mercy.

Ref: *Jeremiah 29:8-14*

FROM AN EIGHT BALL TO A DESTINED CALL

Likewise the Spirit also helpeth our infirmities: for we know not what we should pray for as we ought: but the Spirit itself maketh intercession for us with groanings which cannot be uttered. And he that searcheth the hearts knoweth what is the mind of the Spirit, because he maketh intercession for the saints according to the will of God. And we know that all things work together for good to them that love God, to them who are the called according to his purpose. *Romans 8:26-28 KJV*

Doors began opening very early in my life that allowed the enemy access to house many spirits within me. But, the one spirit that was the hardest to shake was the spirit of bondage.

At the early age of ten years old, I began stealing cigarette butts out of the ashtray. I picked dried brown grass out of the yard to roll up and smoke. I can even remember a few times when I used oregano for marijuana (pot). I would make myself believe that I was getting "high." (This is how doors are opened in our lives and the lives of our children. Be very careful of what you expose your children too.)

By the time I was thirteen, I was smoking pot and cigarettes as well as drinking alcohol on a regular basis. I did not realize I would one day regret ever taking the first pull off either one. (Once the door of the drug spirit is opened, you are exposing yourself to many other spirits because drugs alter your mind.)

As time went on, I continued down the reckless path that would eventually bring much pain into my life. This reckless behavior would also cause me to make bad choices and lose many assets.

By the time I was eighteen, I was not only smoking and drinking but was also being exposed to cocaine. Cocaine, my friends, is another devil on a whole new level. (Take heed to the friends that your kids are around, what may appear innocent is not always innocent.) This all began as a trial. I started out buying a "dime bag" equating to $10 worth of cocaine. I progressed to buying an "eight ball" bag which totaled $100 almost every day. I can only describe it as starting out with a loose rope around my neck. I believed I could slip that rope off at any time. However, the rope had a chain and padlock which had me bound for the next eighteen years of my life.

The thing that I would like to point out in this testimony is how the enemy tricked me to believe that I was always in control of my drug use. For a short period of time, I was in control. Satan kept telling me that I could stop at anytime I wanted. One day I began to realize that I was getting in over my head with bills. I was working everyday but I had nothing to show for it. Bill collectors were calling, my credit was being destroyed, I was at risk of losing my job, and a lot of other pressing issues were taking place in my life. I decided that I would stop! Just…Like…That! WRONG!!!

The enemy began to attack my mind. Satan was fine as long as I was living for him. But, as soon as I made a decision to stop, I began to see things. I would see and feel things crawling on my body. I had anxiety attacks. I was paranoid – always looking out of the window at all times of the night. I thought I was going to die in my mess. But GOD! He delivered me! He brought me out of an eighteen year drug habit without rehabilitation. I am a living witness! Today, I let you know that with God all things are possible. All you have to do is surrender your life to Him. He will do the rest for you.

If you are reading this testimony, it is because God wants you to know that you do not have to be bound by the evil things of this world. It may not be drugs or alcohol, but whatever it is give it to Jesus Christ on today. Let go and let God into your life completely. Christ stands at the door knocking. Will you let Him in to set you free?

Ref: II Corinthians 4:8-18

I CAN SHOW YOU BETTER THAN I CAN TELL YOU

Dearly beloved, avenge not yourselves, but rather give place unto wrath: for it is written, Vengeance is mine; I will repay, saith the Lord. *Romans 12:19 KJV*

All the signs were there from the beginning but I was too blind to see them. I was just coming out of depression. My mom passed when I was sixteen years of age. I had not properly coped with her death. When I graduated from high school, I entered college. I even stayed in the dorm. However, I never made it through my first semester. I remember feeling so tired one day I left school. I found myself down at my grandparent's house. I was tired and angry! I tried to leave but my car would not start. I remember thinking my grandfather sabotaged my car. As I look back, I now realize it was the hand of God protecting me from ending my life. I was suicidal. Well, my depression got worse and through a series of prayers and intimate counseling I was on the road to recovery. That is when I met "the one" whom I felt and knew God had sent me. I thought and felt I was in love. But how could God truly have sent someone to me when I did not love myself or God fully?

We started dating while I was still dealing with depression. I was very up front and honest about my condition. There seemed to be a level of acceptance towards it.

After a period of time, the "true" person started manifesting. I felt uncomfortable in this situation but I did not know how to end things. I was lied to but I chalked it up as everyone had issues; I would just look beyond them. This was all while we were dating. So what did I do? I got married.

I sold my house and land to help "us" get into a new home. Just before the closing, I checked the account and the money was gone. It turns out that my spouse had withdrawn it. I was mad but I accepted it. Like I said, all the signs were there but I ignored them.

The enemy was attempting to break me. He was trying to make me so weak that I would give up my very life. But GOD kept me even through the storm. The worse my circumstances became the more I went to church and praised and worshipped God. It was in that time God began to truly deliver me from depression and strengthen me to stand and endure that season of my life.

We argued and I endured. However, I grew tired of arguing would disengage myself. God was moving in my life. I kept on praying! I would ask about praying together but the response was always that prayer did not work.

Noticeable signs of infidelity were appearing; however, I was accused of cheating.

Money continued to be removed from the account and bills were past due. I started secretly asking for help from the church.

The last incident was Christmas Eve. After being called stupid in the "argument of the hour" I replied, "If it wasn't for being negative there would not be anything to say." Things rapidly went downhill from there. Law enforcement was called. Yet, God still had His wall of protection around me.

I later realized after the divorce and truly being delivered from depression that I was never in love. I lied on God saying He placed us together. I realized that we both had issues and needed healing by God. The fault lied in us not aggressively seeking God before we moved forward. I repented. I got strong. I started loving myself and seeking God's love.

The enemy was trying to keep me down and out. But God heard the prayers of the saints crying out on my behalf. The enemy wanted to keep me in the state of accepting abuse and defeat. But I read in God's Word where He said vengeance belonged to Him. I developed an "I can show you better than I can tell you attitude." I stubbornly held on to God's unchanging hand and would not let go. I was in a tug-o-war for my very soul. I thank God because He is Omnipotent. God is always Victorious. In the end, we exchanged apologies and forgave one another. I truly understand that with God we ALL become new creatures in Him. The past is the past. If refuse to allow my past to deter my future.

Ref: Matthew 6:25-34

Summation of a Testimony

Each person was asked to give at least two of their favorite Scriptures. As you read the testimonies, these Scriptures were perfectly fitting for each test encountered. It then becomes conclusive that the Bible, the very Word of God is alive within. They read God's Truth and applied it to their individual lives. Therefore, they boldly proclaim they KNOW it was the mighty, handy work of God that saw them through their test.

Testimonies by the saints are real. They have lived through incident after incident and still remained steadfast and unmovable concerning the Word of God. But as you also read, these tests and trials did not transform them overnight. It was a process. There were many nights filled with grief, tears, and what have you. There were many re-takes on some tests that were failed the first, second, third time. However, they were triumphant through the power of Jesus Christ. You too can be victorious! Give your testimony even before you complete the test. Have confidence in Jesus Christ that He will do exceedingly and abundantly more than you ever expected in your life. Apply pressure on God by giving Him His Word back. God honors His Word.

Father God in the name of Jesus, Lord I am ready to be a living testimony. Lord God, I am ready and willing. Father I ask that You make me able to withstand the test. Lord, I realize that there are many tests that I am about to encounter but I believe that by and through Your Omnipotent grace and mercy I will proclaim victory. Jesus help me to give all of my struggles to You never to take them out of Your hand Lord God. Father God, I need Your Holy Spirit to show me the importance of being a living testimony. Lord show me how great it is to share my struggles so that I am not ashamed of all that I have been through. Lord, I desire to share my story, yet I am afraid of being judged by my past. So God, I empty out myself to You Lord God that You may give me Holy Boldness. Deliver me from the opinions of people who hide their struggles. Lord, give me the insight to pray for those people who deny their own testimonies of deliverance. God I know You are able. Lord, show me the way. I am ready Jesus to be a living witness for You Lord God. Lord I am ready to go deeper in Your Word so that Your Word becomes real to me and within me. Lord I am ready to become an ark for You carrying Your commands and precepts. Lord, I am ready to spend more time with You God. Jesus I know and realize that the only way to prepare for a test is to spend time studying. So Lord I am ready to spend time in Your Word. Jesus I am ready to spend more time in Your Holy Presence. Holy Spirit I am ready to surrender and yield to You so that You may show me a more excellent way. Father I pray this prayer in all sincerity and claim victory in being a living testimony. In Jesus' name Amen.

Chapter 6

Cleaning Your Temple

The mountains quake at him, and the hills melt, and the earth is burned at his presence, yea, the world, and all that dwell therein. Who can stand before his indignation? and who can abide in the fierceness of his anger? his fury is poured out like fire, and the rocks are thrown down by him. The LORD is good, a stronghold in the day of trouble; and he knoweth them that trust in him. But with an overrunning flood he will make an utter end of the place thereof, and darkness shall pursue his enemies. What do ye imagine against the LORD? he will make an utter end: affliction shall not rise up the second time. For while they be folden together as thorns, and while they are drunken as drunkards, they shall be devoured as stubble fully dry. There is one come out of thee, that imagineth evil against the LORD, a wicked counselor. Thus saith the LORD; Though they be quiet, and likewise many, yet thus shall they be cut down, when he shall pass through. Though I have afflicted thee, I will afflict thee no more. For now will I break his yoke from off thee, and will burst thy bonds in sunder. Nahum 1:5-13 KJV

Father God in the name of Jesus Christ. Lord I come to You as humble as I know how Lord asking for forgiveness of my sins that I have committed against You Father. Lord I ask right now that You give me Holy Boldness to be an open book to my brothers and sisters who are currently experiencing bondage in their lives. Lord I also ask that You, Lord Jesus, deliver each and every one of us so that we may serve You in all truth. Lord God, thank You for Your precious Son, Jesus, for dying on the cross at Calvary. Lord Jesus thank You for Your precious blood and water. Lord I am thankful that You stayed on the Cross for the remission of my sins. Lord, I am even more thankful that You gave up the Ghost, was buried, and resurrected with ALL power in Your Hands. Father God, I am thankful that You love me, in spite of my mess, that You gave Your only Begotten Son, and that I might even have a Right to Eternal Life. Holy Spirit, continue to purge and build me according to Your Divine purpose and plan for which I have been called. In Jesus' mighty name. Amen.

There is a misconception regarding the Church. First and foremost, WE are the Church. We are temples (arks) of the living God. Yet, so many people consider the physical building in which they fellowship, praise, and worship God to be the only location worthy to be called the Church. Some people get mad about others coming in to the physical building and defiling the Church but they fail to realize that their ungodly lifestyles are defiling the REAL temple God desires to dwell in.

Ref: Romans 12:1-2

People have secret lifestyles. They go to Church and present themselves in one manner. They go to work and present themselves in another. And yet, when they are amongst their friends and family there is still another side of them that they present to people. Which lifestyle truly represents the real person? Most people would state that all of these sides make up the "real me." There is a flaw in two of the three sides. If all of these sides do not adequately reflect a Holy lifestyle, there are definitely issues that are preventing growth in God.

Ref: Luke 16:13

We sometimes come down with a case of the "I can't help it." This mentality gives us a false sense of justification. We go to the physical temple to worship God and leave the same way we came. We have been ill-informed about the REAL temple. The Holy Spirit came to dwell in us. We grieve and upset the triune by not recognizing ourselves as part of the Body of Christ. This "I can't help it" syndrome is caused by extended periods of time ignoring the leading and guiding of the Holy Spirit. The more the instructions of God are ignored, the harder it is to sense His presence.

Once a person becomes numb to the point of total paralysis, the enemy comes in like a flood. It starts with believing one can live their life without any accountability. Denied accountability leads to shunned responsibility. Once they shun responsibility, power and authority given by Jesus Christ is abdicated. Upon abdication of power and authority, their lights are extinguished. If their light is extinguished, total darkness consumes them. Darkness is where evil dwells. In darkness, it is difficult to see the right path to choose. If in darkness, choices are misguided by a warped sense of pull.

The enemy comes to one, steal you away from the fold; two, kill your life force and God ordained connection to the Father; and three, destroy your soul subjecting you to eternal damnation. You cannot afford to be dictated to by the WRONG authority. Your very soul is at stake. This is why it becomes important to clean your temple (ark). You are to present your body and make a sacrifice to God by allowing Him to clean up the secret affairs you withhold from exposing. No one is perfect. The Body of Christ has gone wrong by allowing babes to believe that they have not had to be purged of some filthy habits. This is why "Church folk" are dangerous. Now, do not misunderstand this statement. "Church folk" are pretend Christians. They are the ones who come to church to get the latest gossip as well as to see who was in the church building. These are "Church folk." Their minds have not been transformed from the evil of the world.

There is a battle going on and the war is raging within the mind. Exposure to little foxes has spoiled the crops. Prostrate yourself before God and allow Him to prune you. He is the only one with shears strong enough to sever evil and demonic weeds that have been assigned to choke the very life out of you. This chapter will deal with all those weeds that have exposed you to leading a double lifestyle. These weeds are formerly known as negative strongholds.

Brethren be encouraged in the Lord. Know that God is able to do abundantly and exceedingly above and beyond any dilemma you may be facing. You do not have to remain in a degenerative condition. You can overcome this condition! Trust in God. He is a Master Chemist. He will formulate an ingenious plan of escape for you. He will mix His precious Holy Spirit with anointing, love, kindness, patience, and more to cultivate a high impact concoction that will dissolve any negative stronghold you may be gripped by.

My cousins and I used to play a game entitled, "Baddest Man Hit My Hand." There would be one person in the middle holding out their hands. One person would be standing on the left side and the other on the right. The person who could hit the middle person's hand the hardest would win. The players of the game standing to the left and the right would rear back their hands as far as possible to generate enough force to leave a sting on the middle person's hand. Sometimes the game would be fixed in favor of one person. The person in the middle would move their hand right when a player, whom they did not want to win, was about to make contact. Here's the catch. You only had one shot.

Your situation is in the middle of God and Satan. Satan is standing on the left and God is standing on the right. Satan has been hitting each of your separate situations with all of his might but God is patiently waiting on you to give Him the opportunity to show you He is the "Baddest" person. God will not budge from His ready stance until you invite Him to do so. Are you ready? Give God the go ahead to strike these situations.

Travel with me in the Spirit to see God raising His Hand. Those situations have been hit so many times they are barely recognizable. It appears to have morphed into something else. But GOD has been there every step of the way watching your situation grow into the monster it is now that is controlling your life. Are you ready to allow God to have total control? His hand is coming and it is coming down hard and fast. You can feel the wind from His awesome force. God is serious. He already knows that you have the victory. His magnificent momentum is to prove to you, so that you truly believe, that you are victorious with Him on your side. With just one blow God makes contact with your situation. God's Word carries such a powerful blow to your situation that Satan stands there flabbergasted wondering how it is possible with just one blow. It does not matter how long the enemy has been hitting these situations. It only takes God one time to strike for that situation to line up according to the mighty Word of God. Do not snatch your situations from the strike of God.

All those negative strongholds that have been preventing you from giving God the go ahead shall be rocked to the core. This means the core, the very root of where all of your problems started will be dealt with swiftly by God. He knows how to exert the right amount of force to make you complete in Him. He knows the right amount of strength to apply to make you whole in Him. God loves you! His love does not change based on how much you disobeyed Him. He still loves you just the same. He had you in mind when He sacrificed His only begotten Son. That is how much God loves you. He knew that you would not be able to handle His Judgment so He created Himself in the flesh because He could handle it. That is love. God sits high and still looks on you. He sends forth angels to encourage. He administers correction when we get out of Divine alignment. That is love. No matter how many issues are presenting themselves as negative strongholds in your life God's love is stronger! His hold is Omnipotent.

Ref: Deuteronomy 7:7, 8

While embarking on this journey to discover the Ta'mar Spirit that lies within, we also have to uncover ungodly spirits hiding within. Ta'mar was a virgin. She was pure. However, in today's society people are not afforded the luxury of being shielded at home, confined. They have to leave home to go to school, work, the gym, grocery shopping. As they go various places both good and bad, light and darkness are encountered. People are bombarded with making decisions that affect their future every day. Should a person get even with someone for wronging them? Should one give the middle finger gesture to that person who just cut them off in traffic? What course of action should be taken when the boss is applying undue pressure and not recognizing the hard work already done? What should a person do when they have been lied on, mistreated? With all of these trials, your character is tested. Who are you truly? With good intended lip service, a declaration proceeds forth that "I am a child of God." However, when life throws a curve ball, do you seem to forget who you are and who you belong to.

The enemy is like the neighborhood twenty-four hour convenience store. Demonic forces never close down. Twenty-four hours a day, seven days a week, the enemy is on the job planting seeds.

71

These seeds are called negative Strongmen seeds. They serve but one purpose - to steal, kill, and destroy you. You are destined for greatness! Satan knows this and doesn't want to see you walk into your destiny. Therefore, at integral times in your life Satan will assign demonic angels to you to set in motion your self destruction.

With this in mind, become aware and alert every second of the day. Constantly remember who you belong to. Make instant decisions to believe the report of the Lord. Remind yourself that Jesus did not respond the way you may have often times responded when space, time, and territory were threatened. Jesus did not curse people out. Jesus did not lie on people. Our Lord and Saviour did not do evil and contrite things as a means of revenge. The Great Immanuel loved. He covered a multitude of sin with love. He hated the sin. Yet, Christ Jesus loved the sinner. How is your love life?

Ref: Philippians 4:8; Titus 3:1-8

In order to get to this place of LOVE, you have to allow the Holy Spirit to uproot all of the evil demon, spread seeds that has been planted. Acknowledge that on occasion the enemy used you. Within your very being, desire to be used by God. Make a decision that the fence of good and evil will no longer be straddled. Choose the righteous Master. Two masters cannot be served simultaneously.

Ref: Matthew 6:24

Are you ready to discover these negative strongmen and how your life may be "infected?" All infections can be cleared with balm and time. Allow the Holy Spirit to be your balm. He alone can completely heal and soothe any pain and infection. Are you ready for the true and living Spirit of the Lord? He is the Balm!

Ref: II Samuel 13:20

Hold your peace. Do not give regard to whatever it is that has been done to you negatively throughout your life. Dwell in the house of the Father of Peace. Submerge yourself in God and He will birth the Ta'mar Spirit within you. It is time to stop being delusional. Face the inner most secrets which keep you bound. Keep on pressing towards the mark of a higher calling. You can do it!

The Art of Delusion

Sitting in the lecture hall, the professor's voice slowly begins to wan. She cannot seem to keep her mind focused on the seminar. Her thoughts run rampant with how lonely she feels. All of my friends seem to have some semblance of a relationship. Why do I struggle in this area? What is wrong with me?

I am in love with a man who belongs to someone else; sleeping with a man who I will never form a meaningful relationship with. Wow, Bree, she thought to herself, you really need to get a grip girl. I need a plan. Applauds snap her back to the lecturer. She had missed almost the entire speech. But maybe this was a sign. Applauds coinciding with thoughts of a plan was exactly what she needed to do. That solves it. I am going to formulate a plan.

First things first, what am I looking for? ...Hmm? She pondered this question for a moment. Aubrielle Danica Leone what are you really looking for? It is time to get real with you. She pulled out a sheet of paper and momentarily stared at it. A clean slate! Humph, she thought. If it were only that easy to simply pull out a fresh clean sheet of paper with no messy past and let it be used to pursue a new future. "Whatever," she thought. Now, what do I want - what am I looking for? Pen in hand, she thinks, A MAN! Chuckling to herself the lady seated next to her gives an annoyed look. Bree politely stares back and gives her a half-hearted smile. She proceeds to get serious about the list. The lecturer fades and Bree continues to stare blankly at the paper because she realizes that everything within her truly does not know how to begin the list. She feels tainted by life. She wants and desires more but all that is within her is far too polluted. How do I get out of this mess? Every time I get to this point where I am fed up, I seem to give in to that which I know within my heart of hearts is wrong.

Fighting back the tears, she places the blank piece of paper into her purse. A blank slate! Lord please help me to have a blank slate…

I can't move! Why can't I move? Panic gripping every fiber of her being. Looking towards the side of the bed she sees a figure staring at her. Evil! Lord help me! How did it get in my bedroom? It's not very intimidating, she assessed in her paralyzed state. Still can't move. Her eyes close to doze back off to sleep. Gasp! My heart! Bree opens her eyes to see a bigger demon staring at her. It is pacing back and forth. She hears its thoughts. What is so special about her? It peers down at the smaller demon and scolds it. Why could you not finish her off? Why were you so afraid to carry out your assignment? Why is she so special? It reaches out for Bree. She feels her heart pounding ferociously. It feels as if her heart is being pulled out of her chest. She musters the strength to say one word. Jesus! Even calling on the Lord was through much struggle. It felt as if there was a muzzle over her mouth preventing her from fully calling, yelling out the name of Jesus.

The demonic force pulls its hand back and begins to pace again. Still paralyzed she cannot even turn her head like before. She is only able to follow with her eyes. Then it stops and tries again. Bree feels her heart begin to race and pulsate uncontrollably. Again, with great effort she repeats, "Jesus." It pulls back. Just then she catches a glimpse of something else floating above her. This must be an ambush she thinks and feels. Bree realizes instantly that should she die, people will only suspect that she died of a heart attack. They would never know the fight she endured with pure evil. Would the doctors and her family and friends even realize that she was not only too young for a heart attack but also that she was a healthy individual. She begins to sing, "Jesus, Jesus, Jesus," a song often sung in her church. She begins to remember the testimony that even when you cannot say anything you can call on the name of Jesus. Even with an invisible muzzle type apparatus restraining her mouth from completely opening, she fights to speak. She fights for her life, she fights unrelentingly. Finally singing herself to sleep, the battle is over. She has survived another night.

The next morning Bree wakes up and reflects on the events from last night. She quickly pushes what happened aside to begin her day, yet, quickly retreats back to the battle raging within.

Why do people take advantage of my niceness? Play me like I am stupid? Use me to get what they want and then give me their backsides to kiss. How do I break the chain? How do I get them before they get me?

Lord how do I get him back? I believe I am learning my lesson; growing as a person. Looking back, I believe that IF I had just stuck in there with him I wouldn't be going through this pain, misuse, and abuse. All these thoughts rushed through Bree's mind.

On the other hand, maybe both of us needed time apart to grow. Only he grew up without me, he advanced and I didn't. I asked him how he was able to move on. He said he moved around. That truly hurt.

The man truly loves you; but he can't or won't be with you for whatever reason. He was man enough not to hurt me with the real truth of why he doesn't want to try again with me. The more I go through with different men, the more I realize that my heart belongs to him. All I can do is pray and ask God to give me the strength that I need to move on.

The strength to move on..... Move on to what? Lord I need strength right now. I need Your Spirit to lead and guide me like never before. Lord I know it is hard but I need You to show me and more importantly I need the wisdom to understand the GODLY MAN that You have for me. I am tired of engaging the wrong men. Boys trying to be men! Men trying to be "playas!"

I know it is truly time to seek You oh Lord and all of Your righteousness. For if I seek You then I know that I am not only seeking right, but also the right thing, person, and direction in my life.

Help me Father. Bree closed out her prayer knowing that she needed the Lord more than ever...

The Illumination

Ref: Psalm 51:10

Can you see when the affects of sincere prayer began to change the situation? The person above is me. I lived within the confines of my mind. I dreamed up the perfect relationship with all of the struggles mixed in with a good dose of reality. Bree was one of the many characters I created in my mind. I would take my life and retreat within my mind to create the very atmosphere I desired manifested. I became a professional at mixing my reality with fantasy which produced a fallacy plagued with depression and confusion. I didn't realize that the very inward manifestation brought forth bad fruit. Even in my imaginations I never got the man. Wow... Talk about your self-defeatist, pessimistic, low self-esteem person living life in bondage.

From the blank piece of paper and creating "Bree," to stating that "I" needed help, no longer was I willing to make believe. As soon as I decided that I needed a Christly change, I encountered the enemy for real! The attack in my bedroom was a real life experience. Although, I wasn't completely cleansed of ALL my sins and corruptible ways, the enemy was alert to the fact that there was another defect. Another soul had started the process of infusing light to all the dark places.

As long as I was on the "dark side," the enemy didn't have to do much to me. I was already playing on his team.

The demonic forces assigned to my life, underestimated my belief. It was due to my sincerity, my cry out for true salvation, and my humble repentance that God heard my cry. In the midst of my filth, God heard my cry!

Ref: Galatians 5:1

Can you see yourself in my former experiences? Maybe you don't have relational problems, or lewd problems, or fornication problems. Therefore, you are possibly thinking this doesn't apply to me. But there are a multitude of sins and vices that the devil uses to gain access to your soul so that he may steal, kill, and destroy you. We believe we are so smart and crafty. Because a person doesn't mention the EXACT sin we are wallowing in, we reject the message of true salvation, grace, mercy, and repentance. We even are so bold as to thumb our nose down on the person shedding light on the darkness they have encountered.

Ref: Galatians 5:7-9

Read Galatians 5:16-26, to see more vices of evil, self-destructive bondage.

In order to live a life completely sold out to Jesus, we have to completely sell out. Every weight or sin that easily besets us or gets us off track, we must submit to God that the Spirit of God purge us. Because some of us have been in the world longer than we have been saved, we have to truly shift our ways of living to Holy living. It does not happen with the blink of an eye like a magical Genie. God is not a magician! You are going to have to work for it. You have to pray, seek His face, study His Word, and yes fast.

How is your prayer life? Do you start out great and then find that "life" gets in your way? You realize that it has been sketchy in your prayer life. Or, maybe you pray constantly but you are not experiencing the answers to your prayers? What are you praying for? Are you praying for what you want God to give you, instead of praying for God to bless you with what is best for you? Do you really know what's best for you if you are living in the bondage of sin and darkness? Maybe you are a "compromising" pray-er. You tell God you commit to do "do this," if He "does that." God knows the end result. He knew all about you before you were formed in your mother's womb.

What about studying God's Word? Do you read without first praying for direction? Do you read because you know you should, yet, you often wake with the Bible right by your side or actually laying on you? The Bible is a book of instructions and examples of all the struggles you will ever face in life. The Bible is not a book of fictional stories, so stop reading like it is. Start studying it! The Bible is a living breathing document like the Declaration of Independence (I felt that statement all in my spirit, it is worth repeating). The Bible is a living breathing document like the Declaration of Independence. The Bible was relevant when it was written over 2000 years ago and it still applies today. The Bible does not change in meaning. Malachi 3:6a states, "For I am the LORD, I change not." God simply divulges deeper revelations of His Word to us as we live life. The Bible is your very present help in the time of a storm.

Do find yourself in a "Peter and the two sons of Zebedee" situation? Do you fall asleep in the place called Gethsemane? Realize your state and move forward! How can you say that you pray or read when you cannot even stay awake? You will never pass the tests of life and you will find yourself going around and around like the children of Is'rael in the wilderness. Wake up!

What about fasting? Ha! Fasting is only for the hard core saints of God. If this is your mindset, it may explain why you are still stuck in mess. I have fasted before. Have fasted, indicates that you are not in the habit of doing so on a regularly scheduled basis. I fast! I give up television, not eating certain things. These are not genuine types of fasting! Do not misinterpret what I am trying to convey to you. God will meet you right where you are. However, you have to do more. As soon as you realize that it isn't a struggle to give up the television or revert to only eating certain foods, then it is time for you to do more. Add on to your method of fasting until you are able to embark on a true fast. I once heard a preacher say, not eating certain foods and calling it a fast is not a fast, but food modification. Search the Scriptures for true fasting, pray to Jesus and allow the Holy Spirit to teach you how to effectively fast.

If God knows all of this about me then why did He allow me to go through this heartache, pain, loneliness, anger, depression, addiction? Why won't He just give me everything I need to pray, study His Word, and fast? God loves you so much; He desires that you have the freedom to choose. Think about it! God gives you the freedom to choose life while the devil binds you and takes away your freedom to choose and causes you to experience death.

Well, this is to serve notice to the enemy. From this point forward choose life. By choosing life, choose God. By choosing God, choose to believe Jesus is the Chief Priest. By choosing to believe in Christ Jesus, choose to live for Him. Choose to invite the Holy Spirit to rest, rule, and abide in your life. Choose to live a Holy life. Choose to be a pure temple for the Holy Spirit to dwell. Choose! The enemy shall no longer keep you from choosing!

Illuminating the Darkness

Ref: Luke 11:20-26

Illuminating or shedding light or Walking in the Spirit of the Word of God means that darkness, satanic forces, and evil have to depart. This does not mean that there will not be a fight!

After reading the above Scripture, realize that the enemy has at some point in your life infiltrated your body and your psyche, and has deposited negative strongmen in an effort to keep you captive.

There are some truths we have to establish and build upon in order to comprehend the bondage of a negative strongman. You have to believe that God created everything. God is always THE FOUNDATION on which to build upon any truth.

Ref: John 1:1-5

The truth is God created everything! Light and dark, good and evil this is all part of God's creation. Do you agree? Let's move forward.

If you believe that light truly exists you have to believe that darkness exists. In a practical sense, when you walk into a room and flip a light switch up, a current of electricity begins to flow and light appears. When you flip the switch down, the light disappears and darkness appears. So is the matter with good and evil. When you flip your spiritual switch off and your light disappears, evil will appear and dominate your life. The Lord acknowledges that evil exists.

Ref: Genesis 2:9

The fall of man happened because of true statements but those statements were not the truth. **True** means "sincere; not deceitful or being or reflecting the essential or genuine character of something." **Truth** means "a verified or indisputable fact, proposition, principle, or the like." While there appears to be no difference between the two definitions, let me give you a simplistic example of true and truth. This illustration was created by an unknown author.

> An atheist, public school teacher was having class one day.
>
> She asked one of her fourth grade students, Johnny, to come to the window. She asked him if he could see the grass.
>
> Johnny answered, "Yes, ma'am."
>
> She asked if he could see the trees, and then asked if he could see the sky.
>
> Again Johnny responded, "Yes, ma'am," to both questions.
>
> Then the teacher asked Johnny if he could see God?
>
> Johnny answered, "No, ma'am, I can't."
>
> The teacher responded with, "Then God doesn't exist. We don't know that any kind of 'God' actually EXISTS!!"
>
> Another student in class, Susie, raised her hand, and the teacher called on her.
>
> Susie asked if she could also ask Johnny some questions.
>
> Amused and curious the teacher consents.

Susie asked Johnny if he could see the grass. She also asked if he could see the trees, and also the sky?

Johnny, who by now was getting bored, answered "Yes," to all three questions again.

Then Susie asked Johnny if he could see the teacher's brain?

Johnny answered with a confused look on his face, "No."

Susie then stated, "Then based on what we have been taught today, the teacher's brain DOES NOT EXIST. Brains do not exist."

Based on this analogy, it was true that Johnny could not see God based on the physical examples given by his teacher. However, it was not the truth. Susie proved it by being inspired by God to use not seeing the teacher's brain as an example. The truth is God exists just like the teacher obviously had a brain.

The enemy tempted Eve with information that was true but it was not the truth. God was protecting the nakedness of Adam and Eve by giving specific instructions. He knew that if they would be partakers, they were certain to face death. Yet, they were disobedient.

Jesus is the TRUTH!

Ref: John 14:6

But we operate outside of His Will when we concentrate on the things that are true. It may be true that your current condition may be an addict, adulterer, fornicator but the truth is God in His infinite wisdom sees past your condition and tells you the TRUTH of who you truly are in Him.

Ref: I Peter 2:9; Philippians 2:15; Psalm 139:14

So the TRUTH is that your ways are not pleasing to God. However, God loves you unconditionally. God's love does not waver based on your actions or inactions. Repent, for the

Kingdom of God is at hand. You are not a lost cause. You may simply be in a backslidden state. This is what God has to say to the backslider.

Ref: Jeremiah 3:14

If you are not saved, please KNOW and live in this TRUTH. You are not a lost cause. You simply need to surrender your life over to God.

Ref: Acts 2:38

Maybe you are in the extreme condition of a backslider condition. What must you do? Repent!

Ref: II Peter 3:9

Let's review. We know and understand that God created everything and He is the foundation, God's Word mentions evil, there is a difference in true and truth, God is TRUTH, and we should operate, function, and live in TRUTH. This truth leads us to His marvelous light. We also know that we are not addicts, fornicators, and so forth, we are images of God Almighty. We are called "Sons of God." It is with this knowledge that we move on to delve into "Negative Strongmen" attempting to keep us in bondage. I used the word "attempting," because your situation is only temporary if you desire to earnestly seek God and ALL His righteousness. Take note that I also stated, "If you desire." In other words, you have to choose!

Ref: Deuteronomy 30:19

Let's press! Press towards God!

> Father God in the name of Jesus. Lord, once again I come to You humbly bowed asking forgiveness of sins committed against You. Lord I not only ask forgiveness but I also repent and turn from my evil and wicked ways. Jesus, I turn to you from evil. Holy Spirit, shine Your marvelous light on as well as in my life and expose all areas of darkness. Father God, I am tired of living a double lifestyle. Holy Spirit, I hunger to be illuminated

and submerged in Your light. Lord God, I desire to live whole heartedly for You. Lord teach me. Lord God keep me hidden in Your LOVE as I go through this transformation. I plead the precious blood of Jesus over every negative strong man secretly hiding in darkness lying in wait setting a net of deception for me. Lord God, in the mighty name of Jesus I take authority rightfully bestowed upon me and bind all situations, circumstances, and conditions not of You. Lord Jesus it is with this authority that I declare and decree, "The Lord rebuke thee Satan!" to all evil manifestations. Holy Spirit, cut off and uproot up all manner of evil fruit. Renew my mind Lord on an ongoing basis. Create in me a clean heart and renew a right spirit within me. Lord, You see my hurt. Nevertheless, Lord Jesus I press on towards You. Jesus I turn my lifestyle over to You. Lord, even when things seem to be getting worse because I desire to get it right with You, I still decree that I will press my way to You. Lord God, I understand more and more that my test will be a testimony to set captives free. Lord, I am more than a conqueror in You. Thank You, Holy Spirit for lighting up my life. Thank You Holy Spirit for teaching me Your ways. Thank You, Spirit of the Living God for uprooting that which produced bad and evil fruit in me. Thank You Jesus for depositing in me Your spiritual fruits grounded in TRUTH. I pray this prayer in Jesus' name. Amen.

Chapter 7

Exposing Negative Strongmen

But if I with the finger of God cast out devils, no doubt the kingdom of God is come upon you. When a strong man armed keepeth his palace, his goods are in peace: but when a stronger than he shall come upon him, and overcome him, he taketh from him all his armor wherein he trusted, and divideth his spoils. He that is not with me is against me; and he that gathereth not with me scattereth. When the unclean spirit is gone out of a man, he walketh through dry places, seeking rest; and finding none, he saith, I will return unto my house whence I came out. And when he cometh, he findeth it swept and garnished. Then goeth he, and taketh to him seven other spirits more wicked than himself; and they enter in, and dwell there: and the last state of that man is worse than the first. Luke 11:20-26 KJV

Luke clues us in on how evil spirits work. The question then becomes what types of evil spirits are there? Coming into this knowledge, you have to understand that there are specific names for evil spirits. It is not enough to simply state evil spirits. Because of our own understanding if we fail to "think" of something evil in our lives then that spirit runs and hides in the darkness that still exists. We have to be specific! If we lie, then we need to expel the "Lying Spirit" by the blood and authority and power of Jesus Christ. This is how we get better. We don't hide behind wanting help but not stating the specifics or areas we need help in.

If you go to the doctor and find that your blood pressure is high, and the doctor gives you a prescription without specifying the proper dosage, that is dangerous. There is a process. The doctor asks you if you are temporarily under some type of stress. He instructs you to monitor your pressure and report back within a week. When you come back, your pressure is taken aga' `'-re is no change he prescribes medication at a dosage co your pressure level. He instructs you to come back in weeks. When you return to the doctor's office, yo checked to verify whether or not the dosage prescrif

If not, then based on your blood pressure reading, the doctor either decreases or increases the dosage. Do you understand why being specific is so important? Being vague is detrimental to your health, your livelihood!

While working on this book, the song playing in the background is truly God's inspirational timing. The lyrics to the song are, "Giants do die. The bigger they are. The harder they fall." They go on to sing, When you shout, they gotta come down."

The next song's lyrics state, "Right, I just wanna be right. When you see me walking along, I just wanna be right."

How fitting are these lyrics to begin dealing with negative strongmen. These giants have to come down because we want to be right with the Lord. Praise God! Go ahead, get your praise on! Rejoice because God is already moving on your behalf. God is already shining His light on you to fill you! Hallelujah! Glory be to God!

This next section will only cover sixteen negative strongmen that manifest specific evil spiritual fruit. Serving God in Spirit and Truth takes on deeper meaning when a person understands that there is more than God's Spirit that exists. **Spirit** is defined as, "the disposition or influence which fills and governs the soul of anyone; the efficient source of any power, affection, emotion, desire." Seek out God fearing prayer warriors in the church to help you in the process of cleaning out your temple. Go down in prayer and fasting. Call upon the elders of the church.

Ref: Matthew 18:20; Mark 9:29; James 5:14-16

The Seducing Spirit

I am the seducing spirit. I deceive and tell hypocritical lies, my conscience is seared. I am attracted to false prophets, fake signs and wonders. I seduce and fascinate people by evil ways, objects, and people. I can entice people to wander away from the Truth of God. I am the seducing spirit.

Seducing signifies a continual state. **Seducing** means, "to cause to stray, to lead astray, lead aside from the right way." Taking the root word, **Seduce** means, "wandering, roving; misleading, leading into error, a vagabond, tramp, imposter, corrupter, deceiver."

Ref: *II Timothy 4:1-2; Revelation 2:20; Luke 10:19; John 16:13; James 4:7*

The Familiar Spirit

I am the familiar Spirit. Astrology, fortune telling, and horoscopes are my tools of choice. I lure people into occults. I operate in mediums and clairvoyants. When you indulge in drugs I create the hallucinations you see. I thrive in the passive dreamers mind. When you lose focus of God, I am there to give you distractions to focus on. I give out false prophesies and speak in false tongues. I am the familiar spirit.

Familiar is, "a necromancer, one who evokes the dead; ghost, spirit of a dead one; practice of necromancy; or one that has a familiar spirit; or a soothsayer; a medium."

Ref: *Leviticus 20:6; Deuteronomy 18:9-13; Leviticus 19:31; II Corinthians 10:3-6*

The Perverse Spirit

I am the perverse spirit. I hate God and His Word. I am the one who convinces people there is no God. I thrive off of lust, sexual perversion, and fornication. I am a lover of self twisting the truth to suit my own needs. I am quarrelsome, argumentative even. I wounded you through incest, rape, child abuse, and the like. I stepped in to fill the void with evil actions, foolish mindsets, and doctrinal error. I am the encourager of abortions. I love to abort your God given destiny. I bombard you with effeminate characteristics, pornography, and sodomy. I am glorified when you chronically worry, pollute your mind with filth, live ungodly, and twist the Word of God committing heresy. I am the perverse spirit.

To be **Perverse** is to possess, "crookedness, perverseness, crooked dealing." **Perversion** is, "confusion (violation of nature or divine order); perversion (in sexual sin)."

Ref: Isaiah 59:3; II Peter 2:14-15; Proverbs 14:2; Philippians 2:11-16; I Timothy 6:5

The Spirit of Whoredoms

I am the spirit of whoredoms. I debase the emotionally weak. I destroy self control so you can't refuse sex. I feed you with pornography. I pimp you out spirit, soul, and body. You are my prostitute. Your compromised position affords me to grow within. I am idolatry, love of money, and chronic dissatisfaction. I encourage you to live a worldly life. Who wants to live Holy when you can pig out on food and other indulgences? I am the spirit of whoredoms.

Whoredom is, "adultery, fornication, prostitution; unfaithfulness to God; idolatry." **Whoring** means to, "compromise one's principles for personal gain." While **Whore** is being, "a person considered as having compromised principles for personal gain."

Ref: Hosea 5:4; Nahum 3:4; Ephesians 3:14-19; Ephesians 5:1-7

The Spirit of Bondage

I am the spirit of bondage. I can't call on God. I live in anguish. I do not forgive. I am bitter. I am the spiritual blindness that keeps you in an addiction state. I thrive off of fears. I keep you captive to Satan and bound to sin. You are my servant of corruption. I am the spirit of bondage.

Bondage is, "slavery, the condition of a slave; involuntary servitude; serfdom; or the state of being bound by or subjected to some external power or control."

Ref: Exodus 1:14; Deuteronomy 26:6; Matthew 11:28-30; Romans 8:15; Galatians 5:1

The Spirit of Error

I am the spirit of error. I am un-submissive and un-teachable. I too thrive in false doctrine. My ways are defensiveness, argumentative, and contentious. I embrace the new age movement accepting teachings from all religious and spiritual movements combining them into one. I am the spirit of error.

To **Err** is to, "cause to stray, to lead astray, lead aside from the right way; to go astray, wander, roam about; metaphorically it means to lead away from the truth, to lead into error, to deceive; to be led into error; to be led aside from the path of virtue, to go astray, sin; to sever or fall away from the truth; of heretics; to be led away into error and sin." **Error** is defined as, "wandering, impiety, perversions; error (in morals and religion); confusion, disturbance."

Ref: Isaiah 32:6; Matthew 22:29; II Peter 2:18-22; I John 4:6

The Lying Spirit

I am the lying spirit. Religious bondage is my specialty. I am hypocrisy. I always have opposing ways. I am the church hopper, accuser, gossiper, false teacher, and slanderer. I give false prophesies, sodomize, and I am an adulterer. Homosexuality is my playground. I cause a person to lust. My communication is profane. Divination/witchcraft keeps me flourishing along with superstition. Of course I lie and whisper foolish flattery. I am a strong deceiver. Yes I will deny every accusation. I will do whatever it takes to move ahead from backbiting, to breaking covenants, to extortion. I am the embodiment of vanity. I am the lying spirit.

Lies are defined as, "deception, disappointment, falsehood; deception (what deceives or disappoints or betrays one); deceit, fraud, wrong; fraudulently, wrongfully (as adverb); falsehood (injurious in testimony); testify falsehood, false oath, swear falsely; falsity (of false or self-deceived prophets); lie, falsehood (in general); false tongue; in vain." To **Lie** means a, "conscious and intentional falsehood; in a broad sense, whatever is not what it seems to be; of perverse, impious, deceitful precepts."

Ref: Micah 6:12; John 8:42-47; John 14:6-7; John 16:13

The Spirit of Heaviness

I am the spirit of heaviness. Grief and sorrow, despair and dejection, hopelessness and self-pity are my children. I make you feel alone, gloomy, and rejected. I give you gluttony and excessive mourning as a company keeper. I give you sleepless nights and broken hearts. The weight of the universe is all on your shoulders. I thrive in depression, inner hurts, and despondency which lead to suicidal tendencies. Drink from my cup of bitterness. It will leave you downcast, tired, weary, and bored. I love being burdensome. I am the spirit of heaviness.

Heavy is described as, "to be heavy, be weighty, be grievous, be hard, and be burdensome" or as, "heavy in weight; metaphorically as burdensome; severe, stern; weighty; of great moment; violent, cruel, unsparing."

Ref: *II Chronicles 10:14; Matthew 23:1-4; Isaiah 61:3* **(NOTE: Read Isaiah chapters 61 and 62 to lift the spirit of heaviness.);** *Matthew 11:28-30; John 15:26*

The Spirit of Jealousy

I am the spirit of jealousy. I murder, project cruelty, and cause division. I am anger and rage, revenge and spite. I am hatred. I will debate and cause strife because I am in it to win. I am competitive and contentious. I am restlessness. I covet, am unmerciful, and envious. I am the spirit of jealousy.

Jealousy is characterized as, "sexual passion; ardour of anger, of men against adversaries, or of God against men; envy (of man); jealousy (resulting in the wrath of God)." **Jealous** is, "characterized by or proceeding from suspicious fears or envious resentment."

90

Ref: Numbers 5:14 ; Proverbs 6:34; Exodus 34:11-14; II Corinthians 11:2

The Spirit of Infirmity

I am the spirit of infirmity. Sickness is my breeding ground. Bent body, impotence, frailty, lingering disorders, they are all my hiding places. I oppress leaving one weak. Flaws, defects, and faults are presents from me. I thrive in unsound, unhealthy, and debilitating environments. I am the spirit of infirmity.

Infirmity depicts, "want of strength, weakness; of the body, its native weakness and frailty, feebleness of health or sickness; of the soul, want of strength and capacity" or "a moral weakness or failing; a condition or disease producing weakness; a failing or defect in a person's character."

Ref: Luke 13:11; Romans 6:19; Luke 13:12; John 5:8

The Spirit of Fear

I am the spirit of fear. I torment and provoke horror. I creep into your dreams causing terror and nightmares. I love it when you worry, doubt, and are apprehensive concerning the things of God. Inferiority and inadequacy are my attributes. Timidity, phobias, and lack of trust help me cause anxiety and stress. Fear of man, death and the unseen are wonderful tools I love to use. I can even cause heart attacks. I am the spirit of fear.

Fear is, "terror; dread fear, anxiety, quaking, trembling, (extreme) anxiety, anxious care."

Ref: II Kings 17:25; Job 4:14; Isaiah 66:4; Psalm 56:4; Psalm 111:10; Psalm 139:14; II Timothy 1:7; I John 4:18

The Spirit of Haughtiness (Pride)

I am the spirit of haughtiness/pride. I am self righteous and controlling. I am a rebel and obstinate. I have an abundance of pride and arrogance. I reject God. I am a mocker. I am stubborn and jealous. Witchcraft, gossip, idleness, and scorn keep me in business. I take pleasure in wrath and contention. I am the spirit of haughtiness/pride.

Haughty means to be, "arrogant (bad sense); high, exalted." **Pride** is defined as, "height, exaltation; empty, braggart talk; an insolent and empty assurance, which trusts in its own power and resources and shamefully despises and violates divine laws and human rights; an impious and empty presumption which trusts in the stability of earthly things."

Ref: Psalm 10:4; Proverbs 16:18; Eze'ki-el 16:50; I John 2:16; Matthew 18:4; I Peter 5:6

The Spirit of Divination

I am the spirit of divination. I thrive in drugs and magic. I flourish in fortune telling, soothsaying, stargazing, and horoscopes. Hypnotists, enchanters, warlocks, witches, and sorcerers are my minions. Where there is rebellion and superstition, you can find me. I even dabble in water witching. I am the spirit of divination.

Divination is defined as, "witchcraft, of the nations, Balaam, of false prophets."

Ref: Deuteronomy 18:11, 12; Acts 16:16; Deuteronomy 18:13, 14; Acts 16:18

The Dumb and Deaf Spirit

I am the dumb and deaf spirit. I cause insanity, lunacy, and seizures/epilepsy. Dumbness, foaming at the mouth, gnashing of teeth, and comatose states are in my bag of tricks. I love it when people suffer in silence. I persuade people to self mutilate. Mental illness is where I like to reside causing tearing, crying, blindness, and ear problems. I like it when people gradually fail in health and vitality from grief, regret, and longing. Extreme depression and physical exhaustion are also my handy work. I am the dumb and deaf spirit.

Dumb is described as, "speechless, wanting the faculty of speech." **Deaf** is understood as, "blunted, dull, blunted (or lamed) in tongue, dumb, dull in hearing."

Ref: Mark 9:14-22; Isaiah 29:18; Mark 9:23-29

Spirit of Anti-Christ

I am the spirit of anti-christ. I oppose God and everyone who is of God. I resist the Holy Spirit. I deny the deity of Christ and all His teachings. I am against Christians. I attack the saints' testimonies. I ignore the blood of Jesus Christ. I prosper in legalism, humanism, deception, and lawlessness. I claim that I can bind authority. I will teach you worldly speech and actions. Allow me to educate you on heresies, including speaking in tongues at the wrong time within the body of Christ. I am the spirit of anti-christ.

The **Anti-Christ** is, "the adversary of the Messiah."

Ref: I John 4:3; II John 7; I John 4:1, 2; I John 4:4-6; II John 8, 9

Spirit of Death

I am the spirit of death. Phobias are my area of expertise. From fear of control, ghosts, and funerals I love to cause anxiety and pain. Loss of your dignity brings me great joy. I am the spirit of death.

Death is defined as, "the death of the body, that separation (whether natural or violent) of the soul and the body by which the life on earth is ended, with the implied idea of future misery in hell, the power of death; since the nether world, the abode of the dead, was conceived as being very dark, it is equivalent to the region of

93

thickest darkness, i.e., figuratively, a region enveloped in the darkness of ignorance and sin; the miserable state of the wicked dead in hell; in the widest sense, death comprising all the miseries arising from sin, as well as physical death as the loss of a life consecrated to God and blessed in him on earth, to be followed by wretchedness in hell."

Ref: *Genesis 2:1-4; I Corinthians 15:56; Psalm 23:4; Proverbs 14:27; Eze'ki-el 18:31, 32; I Corinthians 15:50-55*

The Way, The Truth, The Life

Jesus saith unto him, I am the way, the truth, and the life: no man cometh unto the Father, but by me. *John 14:6 KJV*

After reading about these negative strongmen, I am compelled to take this one step further so there is no confusion. God by the power of our Lord and Saviour Jesus Christ can bestow giftings to the saints of God. Looking at these occurrences through carnal eyes will lead to destruction. God is served in Spirit and in Truth. Therefore, we cannot look with natural eyes to determine spirituality. Read I Corinthians 12. This chapter speaks on the various gifts and operations of the Body of Christ. The key is that you have to be part of the Body to truly understand. Seek Godly counsel from God and within the Body of Christ to answer questions. It is imperative we know and understand the Will of God the Father to dispel any confusion that may arise. Remember Jesus is not the author of confusion. Ask the Holy Spirit to open up your understanding so that you may digest Truth, Righteousness, and Holiness. Dare to go deeper in Christ Jesus!

But seek ye first the kingdom of God, and his righteousness; and all these things shall be added unto you. *Matthew 6:33 KJV*

Ask, and it shall be given you; seek, and ye shall find; knock, and it shall be opened unto you: For every one that asketh receiveth; and he that seeketh findeth; and to him that knocketh it shall be opened. *Matthew 7:7, 8 KJV*

Remember your sheet of paper with the list of set ups? Well, in all that you wrote, can you see evil influences? Now is the time to confront those manifestations by the power of Jesus Christ. Declare - NO MORE! No more will I yield to evil influences trying to hinder my progress into my full destiny. No more will I allow demonic spirits to use me! No more will I forget that I have the authority and power by and through the blood of Jesus Christ! No more will I be paralyzed or scared to call on the name of the Lord! No more will I be slack concerning my Father who art in Heaven. No more will I neglect to Hallow His Holy Name.

The Decision

I have to make a decision.
Which way do I now turn?
Do I choose the lighted path?
Or
Do I choose the dark path and burn?

I have to make a decision.
Where do I want to spend eternity?
Do I choose the road less travelled?
Or
Do I choose the road wide with no accountability?

I have to make a decision.
How do I want to spend my life?
Do I choose the tests and share my testimonies?
Or
Do I choose to live a life filled with hidden lusts, struggles, and strife?

I have to make a decision.
There are two roads to choose.
One road, eternal gain.
Or
The other road I'm defeated, I lose.

I have made my decision.
That did not take long at all.
I hear the voice of my Lord Jesus.
No longer will I take heed to the enemy's call.

This is my final decision.
Deciding every second of the day.
I choose to live for Jesus Christ.

Because in Him my life was saved!
By Tiana McGlockton

Heavenly Father I come to You as a meek and humble servant asking for forgiveness for sins I have committed against You Lord God. Father as I have discovered tainted and evil seeds that have been planted in my life I ask right now in the name of Jesus to be purged. Lord I am tired of struggling and never seeming to gain ground. Holy Spirit I need You now more than ever. Holy Spirit I need You to uproot everything that is not like You Lord God. Precious Saviour I ask right now that the portals of the demonic be forever closed in my life. Jesus in Your name I bind all negative strongmen right now. Lord You said in Your word what I bind in earth would be bound in heaven. So God I come to You binding satanic forces. Lord God I loose Your Holy Spirit to reign freely without any restraints in my life. Mighty Father I submit to You and only You Lord. Holy Spirit transform my mind to create a Holy Stronghold in the Word of God. I declare that You are Lord of Lords and King of Kings. Jesus I decree that Your Will shall be done in my life. Lord I thank You for moving on my behalf. Jesus thank You for being the Sacrificial Lamb on the Cross. I ask God that You continue to show me all manner of Spiritual Truth that I may walk therein. I ask and thank You in advance right now Lord. Amen.

Remember when you very badly needed to cry and the tears would not fall. Then one day the tears came and then it seemed as though they would not cease. Afterwards, you felt drained and exhausted. Shortly after that you felt relieved. The release you needed was in your tears. II Samuel 13:20 finds Ta'mar crying just before her brother comes to comfort her. She cried from the time she left Am'non's front door until you find her with her brother Ab'salom. It is at the end of the process where you discover release. Ab'salom, "The Father is Peace," showed up right on time to encourage. Be released to discover the Ta'mar Spirit within you. The next chapter will guide you in releasing "set ups" from negative strongmen.

Chapter 8

Releasing Points

The law is good, then. The trouble is not with the law but with me, because I am sold into slavery, with sin as my master. I don't understand myself at all, for I really want to do what is right, but I don't do it. Instead, I do the very thing I hate. I know perfectly well that what I am doing is wrong, and my bad conscience shows that I agree that the law is good. But I can't help myself, because it is sin inside me that makes me do these evil things. I know I am rotten through and through so far as my old sinful nature is concerned. No matter which way I turn, I can't make myself do right. I want to, but I can't. When I want to do good, I don't. And when I try not to do wrong, I do it anyway. But if I am doing what I don't want to do, I am not really the one doing it; the sin within me is doing it. It seems to be a fact of life that when I want to do what is right, I inevitably do what is wrong. I love God's law with all my heart. But there is another law at work within me that is at war with my mind. This law wins the fight and makes me a slave to the sin that is still within me. Oh, what a miserable person I am! Who will free me from this life that is dominated by sin? Thank God! The answer is in Jesus Christ our Lord. So you see how it is: In my mind I really want to obey God's law, but because of my sinful nature I am a slave to sin. Romans 7:14-25 NLT

Set ups have altered the mindsets of God's people. **Alter** in Greek means **allasso** and is translated "to change, to exchange one thing for another, or to transform." What alters reality is what has been placed on the "altar" of the mind. One meaning of **altar** translated in Greek is bomos. **Bomos** means "an elevated place." It is time to set upon the altar of the mind Holy change. By changing or elevating the mind to the things of God, lifestyles will be set to change for righteous living. Allow God to renew your mind by going deeper into His Word.

Learn what He has in store for you. Tear down those altars of set ups, deceptions, and destruction. Do not let the past affect you negatively. Use your "set ups" as breakthrough testimonies to bring down the enemy's altars. Set someone else up to succeed in Christ! Are you ready?

Father God in the name of Jesus Christ I come to You with Godly excitement. Lord I repent for sins committed against You. Lord I turn and move toward You God. Father I ask that You teach me how to release hindrances that cause me to falter. God transform those hindrances from stumbling blocks to stepping stones. Lord allow the precious Blood of Jesus Christ to be that which holds my life together. In the name of Jesus, I bind every weapon formed against me. I declare and decree that these weapons shall NOT prosper. Lord I submit and yield my mind to You Jesus. I am ready to change Lord. Father create in me a clean heart and renew the right spirit within. Lord, I need a Psalm 51:7 experience in my life. Jesus I ask that You purge me with hyssop and I shall be clean; wash me and I shall be whiter than snow. Jesus I know that if I speak Your Word back to You it cannot return unto You void. So God I stand on Your Word. Mold me into a new creature according to II Corinthians 5:17 so that the old things of my life are passed away. Lord God I desire and seek after You to see all things concerning me become new. It is in the power and authority of Jesus Christ I pray. Amen.

Changing the mindset simply means setting the mind to change. There have been so many evil and negative seeds sewn and harvested. Now your mind has to be trained to reject those evil seeds when the enemy comes to try and re-plant negativity and evil. You must protect your fertile, righteous ground from evil and allow the Holy Spirit to plant fruits of the Father's Spirit in you.

Trust may be an issue. You may be willing but the process of setting your mind presents challenges. So how then can you set your mind to change? Release! Purge those things that hinder you. Let go of all those things that the enemy constantly whispers in your ear. You do not have to entertain evil. You have the option to ignore wicked innuendos. If you have to remove yourself from evil influences, do it. Once your mindset is changed you can go back and witness to those still under bondage by demonic influences. Once you become changed according to God's Word you can effectively minister to people. You can be a living witness that God is faithful.

Releasing Points

God blessed me with the opportunity to minister during the Christmas Holiday in Winter Haven, Florida. The Lord prepared me for this occasion by instructing me to take my study materials on the trip. When asked to minister, I was ready. I began to pray and ask the Holy Spirit what He wanted to minister through me to His people.

I decided to turn the television on and watch the Christian station. While flipping through channels, I saw an old war movie and the title caught my attention. It was entitled "Wake Me When the War is Over." The Holy Spirit quickened my spirit by reading that caption.

God wants His people awake on the battlefield. He does the fighting but He requires that we stand in the battlefield. He began to deal with me and how His people are falling asleep. People do not want to take part in the war in spite of the war raging on in their minds. Yet, they are still battling and struggling.

There is a fight going on whether acknowledged or not. The important question to ask is what armed force employs you? Are you on God's side? Well you should not be asleep. If you are on Satan's side, you can switch forces. Release that evil army fatigue and destroy those weapons of mass, self destruction. All of the self defeatist mental training that you went through can now benefit the Kingdom of God. You can recruit and train for God. You can teach new recruits. You are qualified by your experience. God can use you.

If you are saved, born again, then you need to choose this day whom you will serve. Salvation does not give you a license to live life irresponsibly. You are being watched by lost souls. If these lost souls see that God cannot save you from your mess, then why should they give their lives over to Him? You are an automatic spiritual role model. You are being looked upon for spiritual direction. If you live your life freely allowing sin to reign and dictate your actions lost souls interpret these actions two ways. They either do not believe God can keep them saved because you do not act as if God can keep you or they give their lives to Christ and remain in a posture where sin reigns and dictates their actions. Either way, you have perpetuated a system of spiritual failure in your life and in the lives of those watching you. God is not a failure, but your actions say otherwise. Set your mind to change. Allow the knowledge, wisdom, and precepts of God to be the stronghold inside you. Yield to the Holy Spirit that your lifestyle may be changed to reflect the perfect Will of God.

I turned the television off and began to study by looking up the word wake. To **wake** means "to become active or animated after inactivity or dormancy." The enemy uses people as puppets – pulling their strings to do his bidding. They unconsciously serve Satan with all those negative strongholds dictating their lifestyles. However, a conscious effort has to be made to permit the Holy Spirit to lead and guide you for a Righteous lifestyle. Do you see the difference? Satan dictates and manipulates while the Holy Spirit gives you unction. Look at the dynamics of Jon'adab and Am'non. Jon'adab manipulated Am'non into being a puppet. Jon'adab was the true enemy who manifested demonically in Am'non. "Idleness is the devil's workshop." Never get caught sleeping!

War means "any active hostility, contention, or struggle." You have been dormant to the things of God. It is time to wake up. You have been warring against the Will of God. It is time to be on one accord with God. You have been holding on to situations and using your knowledge to manipulate and spread corruptible seeds. Be incorruptible in Christ Jesus.

I arrived at a point in studying where I needed more answers from God. Once His people were awakened, what would be the next step? He instructed me to turn the television back on. I went back to the old war movie but God wanted me to keep going. Once again, I continued changing channels and stopped on the Christian station but God was telling me to keep going. I ended up on a cartoon television station. This is where I found the next step. I know you may be thinking this is a joke; however, I assure you it is not. God will meet you right where you are. The Holy Spirit knows how to communicate with you. I believe the Lord can and does speak any way He sees fit. I do not limit Christ in where He can reach me. From billboards, to moving cars, to birds, to the essence of nature, to tranquil quiet moments, God desires to be taken out of the nice, neatly wrapped box. If you allow the Holy Spirit to open your spiritual senses, you will see, hear, feel, touch, and smell Him in new and profound ways. God is the God of impossible. Release God from the box. God blessed me with these points just from watching the cartoon.

Fear

Release things or people which cause fear.

Distorted minds cause a lack of genuine reverential fear of God. Reverential fear of God should always be present when serving the Lord.

> So shall they fear the name of the LORD from the west, and his glory from the rising of the sun. When the enemy shall come in like a flood, the Spirit of the LORD shall lift up a standard against him. *Isaiah 59:19 KJV*

> HAVING therefore these promises, dearly beloved, let us cleanse ourselves from all filthiness of the flesh and spirit, perfecting holiness in the fear of God. *II Corinthians 7:1 KJV*

Traumatic and dramatic experiences encountered in the past have affected the present and clouded the future. The enemy has sown seeds that cause fear of everything but God. These seeds must be uprooted.

People fear stepping on cracks, splitting poles, black cats, and the list goes on and on, but do not reverence and fear God as they ought. Some people even fear losing friends because friends have been confidants instead of God. The list could go on and on.

101

In order to progress and obtain the Ta'mar Spirit, a release must take place. Release ALL fear that keeps distance in knowing the truth in the reverential fear of the Lord.

Ref: Proverbs 2:1-9

Am'non feared the unsettled, longing building within himself. He was unnerved by the feelings and urges he had for Ta'mar. With a little coaxing by Jon'adab, Am'non gave in to his impulses. Well beloved, Am'non can no longer harm you in the safety of God. He is your strong tower as well as your fortress. Break the habit of living in negative, unproductive fear. The fear of dogs, the fear of snakes, the fear of spiders, and the fear of heights are all unproductive. These fears, which are not of God, open portals to evil seeds being planted in your life that lead to other negative and unproductive fears.

There is a difference in strong dislike and fear. Strong dislike says I am really uncomfortable but I am not swayed by the obstacle. Fear says not only am I uncomfortable but I am completely paralyzed by the obstacle. Although the line between the two is thin dislike and fear are at opposite ends of the spectrum. A passage of Scripture in Matthew 8:24-27 illustrates that Jesus was peacefully asleep during a storm. He was with His disciples yet they were afraid of the "great tempest of the sea." His disciples had so little faith and so great fear they woke Jesus up to save them. Matthew 14:22-32 shows the courage Peter had to step out of the boat and come to Jesus. However, Peter only made a couple of steps before he allowed fear to grip him. The weight of that fear caused him to sink. Peter feared but it was Jesus who "bid" Peter to "come" to Him.

When Christ died, restoration to Genesis transpired. God from the beginning gave you dominion so why should you fear animals or insects when you have dominion over them? He instructed man to subdue the earth. **Subdue** is "conquering, overcoming, controlling." You cannot subdue when the things of this earth terrify you to the point of immobility. Release those things and people which cause you to be fearful. Fear the living God whole heartedly instead. Reverence the Lord!

102

Pleasure

Release those things and people that give pleasure and leave feelings of guilt.

> The LORD taketh pleasure in them that fear him, in those that hope in his mercy. *Psalm 147:11 KJV*

> For the LORD taketh pleasure in his people: he will beautify the meek with salvation. *Psalm 149:4 KJV*

When a person comes from under the covering of God, he or she is seeking after worldly pleasures. God sends messages and warnings that cause feelings of guilt from indulging in worldly pleasures. The longer one remains in the presence of worldly pleasures the longer they become anesthetized to God sending warning signs. Some people no longer feel guilt any more. They are so numb and warped in thinking. Their lifestyles say God is wrong because the pleasure experienced feels so right. The devil is a lie! This is a wakeup call. Turn away from these guilty pleasures. God can and will show a more excellent way. The pleasure experienced in God far outweighs the arousal experienced in the world.

If you enjoy drinking alcohol, God can give you the experience of being drunk in the spirit. He will have you so full with His Holy Spirit that you will stammer, get weak in the knees, and feel merry and bubbling with joy. God does not give you a hangover or headache the next day. If you enjoy snorting or smoking illegal substances, God can make you high in the spirit. You will see and hear things you have never heard before. You will become so sensitive to the Holy Spirit that you will not want to come down from off of the mountain. If you enjoy intimate relations and you are not married, God can cause you to have such an arousal if you read His Word. He will lead and guide you into deeper depths and higher heights that will leave you breathless. God is a wonder to your soul. If you enjoy using language that is unbecoming of a righteous lifestyle, God can give you a language that will tear down

103

strongholds and electrify the atmosphere. Do you enjoy eating to gluttony? Well God can feed you and make you full of His Word. God does not add pounds but He adds the weightiness of His Word to your life. There are more guilty pleasures that may come to mind. The answer still is and will remain God, God's Word, God's Son Jesus Christ, and God's Holy Spirit. Do not die in a state of guilty pleasures that keep you from serving God in the beauty of His Holiness.

Ref: Eze'ki-el 33:10, 11

Am'non had tunnel vision. His desire for Ta'mar led him to indulge in guilty pleasures. That love for Ta'mar instantly changed to hatred. People go through life hating certain things which have been seen or witnessed. When that person grows older they end up continuing to hate but may find themselves attracted to people who do the things hated. Or, that person may end up doing the very things they claim to hate. It is time to break the generational curse. Indulge in God. Da'vid indulged himself with Bath'sheba and killed her husband Uri'ah just to have her. Am'non followed in his father's footsteps by obsessing over someone and something that was spiritually off limits and out of bounds.

Shame

Release shame that causes depression, anger, or both due to sensitivity in areas of life.

Shame is "a painful feeling of guilt for improper behavior" or "something regrettable or outrageous." Negativity wears down your confidence and brings the onset of shame. Maybe the uniqueness that a person displays was not celebrated but hated. People were unrelenting in causing feelings of being a black sheep, outcast. This could be because those people were possibly not celebrated for their uniqueness.

Because you accepted the fact that your distinctiveness was different from others maybe you have become ashamed. Well, God has a purpose and plan for you. Do not act on improper behaviors which lead to shame or anger. You do not have to take part in regrettable actions. Live for Jesus. There is no shame in serving Him. The outrageous things He will cause you to do will bring about deliverance. The perceived "improper" behavior He directs you to do will break the yoke of religion. Trust God and He will use the sensitive areas of your life to His Glory.

Ref: *Psalm 40:14; Revelation 16:15*

Shame weakens, placing a person under the subjection of bondage which leads further away from Jesus Christ. I read a sign the other day. It stated, "Jesus Christ died for you. So why don't you live for Him?" This is a powerful statement. Do not remain in the posture of shame.

Ref: *Isaiah 54:4, 5*

Am'non was so ashamed by his actions toward Ta'mar that he called for his servant to kick her out of the house. He even told the servant to lock the door. He allowed his passion to bring him to a point of shame. This shame led him to anger. What Am'non did was outrageous. However, do not inflict the bandage of shame where God desires to be the balm that cures you.

Grief

Release the grief that causes suffering with intense emotions by a loss.

Grief is a sickness. Sometimes a person cannot see their present or future because their mind has been trapped by the past. There are events in life that may have caused feelings of intense emotions because of a loss of someone or something. This person cannot get past bearing the pain from the occurrence. Grief can lead to depression. Depression takes one down dark paths if not handled properly. Grief keeps picking at the covering of a wound so that it does not heal. Grief is that constant reminder that a person has undergone a loss in life.

As long as you live you will experience some type of loss. Do not remain in the grief department. Find a positive and uplifting place to shop. Go visit the joy and happiness departments.

> Be ye angry, and sin not: let not the sun go down upon your wrath: Neither give place to the devil. Let him that stole steal no more: but rather let him labour, working with his hands the thing which is good, that he may have to give to him that needeth. Let no corrupt communication proceed out of your mouth, but that which is good to the use of edifying, that it may minister grace unto the hearers. And grieve not the Holy Spirit of God, whereby ye are sealed unto the day of redemption. Let all bitterness, and wrath, and anger, and clamour, and evil speaking, be put away from you, with all malice: And be ye kind one to another, tenderhearted, forgiving one another, even as God for Christ's sake hath forgiven you. *Ephesians 4:26-32 KJV*

When you linger in grief mode, you act out of Godly character and become weak and immobile in your lifestyle. The Bible declares that the joy of the Lord is your strength according to Nehemiah 8:10. If you are grieved and weak, then you are not finding joy in the Lord your God. He will give you strength. Snap out of it! Grief keeps company with tragedy and sorrow. Get some joy in your life. Joy will cause you to clap your hands, leap for joy, pat your feet, celebrate victory, and enjoy personal triumph in God. Once you understand this kind of joy you will wonder why you were grieved so long.

Ref: Psalm 31:9-18

Am'non caused Ta'mar to grieve. The violation was unthinkable of a loved one. Am'non created a wound in Ta'mar that appeared beyond repair. Ta'mar tore her clothes and placed ashes (dust) on her head from the grief. She had lost something so precious. Yet, her brother Ab'salom came along. Remember his name means the Father is Peace. Before Ta'mar could get further down the road in her grief, the Father stepped in and offered her peace in the situation. The Father instructed her to think no more on what happened. He wanted her to dwell in peace. Think not of the things of old, dwell in peace. The Father wants you to.

Lies

Release lies that were meant to deceive.

The source of lies is spawned from Satan. He is the father of lies. Satan will use anyone who will allow themselves to be used as a vehicle to spread lies to stop the progress of building the Kingdom of God. No one is so special that people will not lie on them. One cannot stop people from lying. A person can only live an open lifestyle of truth according to the Gospel of God. To combat lies, live a lifestyle of truth grounded in the Word of God.

> **Blessed is that man that maketh the LORD his trust, and respecteth not the proud, nor such as turn aside to lies.** *Psalm 40:4 KJV*

> **A false witness shall not be unpunished, and he that speaketh lies shall perish.** *Proverbs 19:9 KJV*

You cannot be in the presence of the Lord and tell lies. You cannot lie to yourself believing you are in great standing with the Lord and your lifestyle is wretched. Allow Christ to reveal your true standing in Him. Do not be alarmed by what He shows you. With Jesus Christ at the helm of your life, you can be transformed and changed. He will show you how you truly are and then work on you all while hiding you in Him. He is your refuge. God is your strong tower. He is a fortress. Do not lie to people. Find a way to tell people the truth so that they may receive correction, repent unto God, and move forward. Lies keep you running in place never moving forward. Lies are spoken as truth but actions are the revealers of truth. People often quote, "I am blessed and highly favored." Then they are seen behaving in ways that are not blessings to them or anyone around. There is no such thing as fake it until you make it in Christ. Jesus was not a faker and neither should you be one. To be fake and phony is a lie. If there is a pressure then remain silent. You do not owe an explanation to anyone but God and the authority figure He has set you under.

107

Learn how to stand your ground and choose silence over lying or lies.

Ref: Ephesians 4:12-16

Am'non lied to get close to Ta'mar. Am'non allowed himself to believe the false counsel of Jon'adab. He wanted to trust in a lie because that trust would allow him to be with Ta'mar. Am'non knew that Ta'mar was not to be touched or handled wrongly. He did not care because he was operating on lies. His vision was clouded by a web of deceit. He began to believe the lies he had told because the end result was forbidden pleasure.

You do not have to lie anymore. God knows your true condition. Submit and yield to the Holy Spirit and be renewed. You do not have to believe lies anymore. Jesus Christ will direct you in all truth. He will be your warning signal when something or someone should not be believed. He will reveal the truth of the nature of every situation that arises concerning you. The Lord will reveal all true intentions when He sees that it is necessary. Trust in God, not Satan, the father of lies.

<u>Insight</u>

Release the insight that causes an illusion of separation.

I once heard a preacher say, "Saved people live in or go through hell on earth and take comfort in passing through this life to eternity and joining Christ in Heaven. While the unsaved believe they are living life as if already experiencing heaven and when they die they will go straight to hell."

There is a two-fold lesson into insight.

First, those born again are sometimes disillusioned to think that hardships will not be encountered. After all, they are saved and live for Christ. However, there is a transitional period in a born again believer's life where they have a feeling of wanting to return to the world because life seemed easier living a life of sin. This person has failed to realize that when they lived a hell bound life in Satan; he had no need to cause duress. The minute salvation was received there was an upset in the balance of the universe. Another victory was counted in Heaven.

The enemy is mad that you have changed sides. He wants you back! However, now there are angels assigned by God to you that war on your behalf. So you must go through. Be purged of the illusion of separation.

> **My sheep hear my voice, and I know them, and they follow me: And I give unto them eternal life; and they shall never perish, neither shall any man pluck them out of my hand. My Father, which gave them me, is greater than all; and no man is able to pluck them out of my Father's hand. I and my Father are one.** *John 10:27-30 KJV*

Second, those who are yet lost believe they are separate from God because they have not professed Christ as their Lord and Savior. There is an illusion of separation due to spiritual blindness. Unbelievers have hard hearts and will not allow God to penetrate them with the light of truth. Unbelievers live destructive lifestyles because they have not been revealed the truth of God. The truth is that God is still faithful regardless of sinful natures. The truth is that God still loves in spite of.

> *Ref: John 3:16-21*

Satan did not and will not lay down his life for anyone. God wrapped himself in flesh to dwell amongst His people. He knew He was the only one capable of paying the ultimate price to return and restore His people to their rightful positions in the Kingdom. The enemy tried to disillusion Jesus Christ by offering a twisted sense of reality. However, Jesus knew the enemy did not have authority or the power of God His Father. Jesus defeated the devil's attack by speaking the Word of Truth which comes from God. This is the only way to defeat the enemy and satanic attacks. You cannot live for Christ and have no insight into the Word of God.

Insight is literally the "ability to see and understand clearly the inner nature of things." Insight in the Bible deals with discernment. To **discern** means "to perceive or recognize clearly." According to Scripture, to **discern (ra'ah)** means "to see, look at, perceive, consider." You must be able to determine the Will of God for your life through Scripture and divine inspiration from messengers of Christ Jesus. Realize that in the beginning God created the heavens and the earth. From the beginning God created man in His divine image. Know that God created male and female. You must discern the truth of who your Creator is according to the Word. Understand the motivations behind the actions, thoughts, and behavior being exhibited in and around you. Insight also deals with understanding. To **understand** means to "be thoroughly familiar with; to grasp the importance, significance, and implications of." You gain understanding and discernment through going deeper into the Word of God. You grow in God and you grow in the underlying Truth of God at all junctures in life.

Ref: Psalm 119:104, 105; John 14:1-4; Hebrews 5:13, 14

Am'non was given the wrong insight which caused him to have an illusion of separation. In one statement he stated his "brother Ab'salom's sister" and in the next statement to manipulate his father Ta'mar was "his sister." Am'non was using wicked and deceitful insight to gain something and someone that was not his to possess. He behaved as a fool by following the advice of the wicked counsel of Jon'adab.

"THE earth is the LORD's, and the fullness thereof; the world, and they that dwell therein. For he hath founded it upon the seas, and established it upon the floods." Psalm 24:1, 2. God created you from within Himself. Return to your Creator. Do not continue to live separate from Him. Destroy the illusion of separation.

110

Attachment

Release attachments to the world and worldly possessions and pleasures.

Let's face it. Living worldly was a blast! Life was heaven on earth. However, the reality of the fact is that one should rather live in hell on earth so that they will not miss heaven. Coming out of the world presents many challenges. A person has to deal with people continuing to live worldly lifestyles. One cannot live life as a hermit never coming out. Although a person may go through transitional periods of being hidden by God, that is a different matter completely.

You are supposed to be a light to the world. **Attachment** simply means "devotion." **Devotion** is "loyalty or deep affection." What are you attached (devoted) to that prevents you from given up wicked, worldly ways? These ways that are not of God are not worth dying in sin and spending eternity in hell. The Bible does warn about holding onto worldly lusts. There is no once saved, always saved. Lucifer was one of God's chief angels. He was in charge of worship. If Lucifer and one third of all the angels were kicked out of heaven by God, then no one can live according to the world's measures and still remain saved.

Ref: Acts 17:23, 24; Romans 1:28-32

There is a battle going on in the mind. Worldly information and Godly information are jockeying for lead position. The enemy wants you to continue attaching yourself to the drugs, alcohol, lusts because you worship him by continuing to be disobedient to God. By the Blood of Jesus, God loves you so much that there is a war for you. God keeps placing people with testimonies in your life to help you realize you can be delivered from worldly attachments. Whose mark do you have on your head? God has His angel marking His people. Satan also has his demonic angels doing the same. Consider why the alcohol, drugs, and all those other habits are more important to you. It is time to stop being in denial. Too many of God's people have been delivered for you NOT to believe that you can't be delivered. Give up those worldly attachments you are devoted to and worship which cause you to be bound by the enemy. To loose the bands of wickedness is to speak God's Word over your life and put actions behind God's Word.

Ref: Romans 12:1-5

Make God your attachment. Now this type of attachment is healthy and beneficial. Attach your ways to God's ways. Attach your thoughts to God's thoughts. Attach and devote your life to seeking after God. The Scripture says to taste and see that the Lord God is good. If you have a taste for unhealthy, evil things, try Jesus. You will see that He does taste good.

Am'non was attached to an evil thought and he carried out a plan that would destroy more than one life. But God stepped in and told Ta'mar to remain in peace. Am'non on the other hand lost his life. Am'non was next in line to be King. Yet, his distorted, wicked attraction to violate Ta'mar caused him to forget his place in the Kingdom. Ab'salom murdered Am'non, fled from the kingdom, and conspired against his father. In the end Ab'salom lost his life. King Da'vid mourned, grieved, and was punished by God at the end of II Samuel 24. This lets you know that no one is above deceitful attachments, trickery, and treachery. We must all be on guard at all times.

God is saying that Am'non will get his just reward for violating you. Do not dwell in why Am'non had a wicked attachment to you. Permit Ta'mar to be an example. Remain in the Father's house in peace. Move forward in God. Attach your motives, ways, thoughts, lifestyle to Him.

Tying Release Points Together

These seven release points if not taken seriously will ultimately lead to destruction. Whatever the addiction, be it substance, material, physical it all started with some type of fear not of God. The Greek word for **fear** is "phobos." Does that look familiar? Phobia is what is recognized as dealing with a myriad of fears.

112

There is sometimes no type of fear when it comes to God. The enemy has confused the mind and thought patterns of many. Can God truly handle messed up minds? Do not be fooled. God has all power. Do not run from God for fear of Him seeing your true condition or state of mind. God already knows and sees your current condition. But He still loves you and wants to clean you up. Stop fighting God and instead fight the enemy with the Word of God. Do not be afraid of changing because people who are still in the world KNOW all your dirt. Forget them. God can use you to deliver them. You have to release negative fear. Run to God; fall down and repent. He will pick you up, dust you off and set you up to be an example of His power. Reverence God and fear Him.

Out of fear of God, No'ah built the ark, A'braham offered I'saac as a sacrifice, Ja'cob wrestled with the angel of the Lord, and Eze'ki-el prophesied to dry bones.

If No'ah had not built the ark, he would have died in the flood which did not manifest until 120 years later. No'ah's name means "rest." It was two-fold. No'ah did not rest until the job was complete and God gave No'ah rest for being obedient. Think about how people must have talked about No'ah. Yet, he obeyed God. He didn't allow fear to creep in and alter his thinking that there would be no flood. No'ah's mind was set on God. Release beloved!

I'saac was the only begotten son of A'braham and Sa'rah. I'saac was the son that God promised to A'braham. A'braham's name means "father of a multitude." If A'braham did not follow through with presenting I'saac as a sacrifice, A'braham would not have become the father of many nations. A'braham messed up numerous times but he obeyed God. A'braham's mind was set on honoring the instructions of God. Release beloved!

Ja'cob mischievously conned his brother out of his birthright for a bowl of stew. Ja'cob's name means "follower." Ja'cob ran away, was mistreated by his uncle, decided to return home, and made peace with his brother. Ja'cob ran but he could not hide. He was compelled to follow where God was leading him. It was during the journey back home that Ja'cob wrestled with the angel of the Lord.

113

Out of fear of not being blessed, he would not let go. The angel touched his hip to move it out of socket but Ja'cob would not let go. As a result, his name was changed to Is'rael. **Is'rael** means "the prince that prevails with God." He prevailed indeed and became the father of the twelve tribes of Is'rael. Ja'cob would not allow fear of what would happen between him and E'sau stop his progress. He returned to the place where he transgressed with a repentant heart. Ja'cob's mind was stayed on God. Release beloved!

Eze'ki-el was a prophet of God. Eze'ki-el's name means "God strengthens." He was deported to Bab'ylon early in his life. Eze'ki-el ministered and prophesied while he was in exile. The method of infiltration was to bring the Jews to Bab'ylon and allow Bab'ylonians to creep into and change their mindset. But Eze'ki-el kept prophesying and warning. He warned them of the approaching destruction of Jeru'salem. God kept strengthening. The end result is that the Jews were not swayed by idolatry while living in an idolatrous country. Eze'ki-el could not fear the captors' faces. He had to preach the Word of God. Release beloved!

There are so many more examples of men and women who had the proper fear. They feared the Lord. But, the wrong type of fear leads to indulging in guilty pleasures. Remember the city of Sod'om. Because of their indulgence of evil pleasures, God destroyed everyone and everything associated with the city. Lot's wife looked back on the city and turned into a pillar of salt. Guilty pleasures are tied to your emotions. Emotions are deceitful. **Emotions** are "strong feelings." **Feelings** are "physical sensations." The addictions to guilty pleasure are associated with physical stimuli. The truth of God lies in spiritual stimuli. Your emotions will lead you astray. Release beloved!

If people knew the depths of your indulgence they would be ashamed of you. This may be the thought which led you to shame. Shame may have made you feel unworthy because of the state of your condition. After disobeying the command of God, Adam and Eve realized they were naked and grew ashamed of their condition. They only realized they were naked because they stepped out of the Will of God by disobedience. Disobedience is also known as lawlessness. The "feeling" of shame comes from disobedience of God. This feeling has people in bondage but God can and will cover and clothes each and every person with His righteousness. He is compelling you to come into the ark of His safety. He is able to hide your nakedness. The enemy wants you to continue being ashamed because he wants to destroy you.

If you do not take heed from the inception of shame, grief will show up. Grief causes affliction to the body. Grief torments. The inward, unexpressed heartache felt leaves sorrow and burden. The ultimate inspiration for handling grief is found in I Chronicles chapter 4. In the middle of the Scripture we find a man by the name of Jabez. The prayer of Jabez is one of the most powerful prayers ever written. His mother bore him in sorrow; hence his name was to be Jabez. As Jabez grew he became a very prominent figure. He was said to be embarking on an important and critical service. He knew, in spite of grief and sorrow, that God would deliver and answer prayer. In the midst of his trials, Jabez prayed. At the end of his prayer, it states that "God granted him that which he requested." Do not allow grief to conquer and leave you defeated. God will grant you breakthrough if you push through your grief. Release it now in the name of Jesus!

With "if" being the operative word, the grief of not being able to control oneself leaves devastation. It causes people to take matters into their own hands. They begin to lie - Feeling as if they couldn't possibly face the truth. Some never realize that they are not lying to man but to God. In Acts chapter 5, a man by the name of Ananias and his wife Sapphira died for holding back and lying. When lies are told death occurs. The more lies told the greater the risk losing oneself completely. It could even get to the point of not knowing the truth from a lie.

Lies bring a deeper misconstrued insight. This leads to living a double life; becoming a person with multiple personalities. When in the presence of the pastor, you act one way. When with friends in the streets, you act another way. Yet when by yourself, you act another way. Which person is the real you? It is impossible to clearly understand the truth of God when insight is split. Judas Iscariot betrayed Jesus for a lack of spiritual insight. His mind was

115

on selling Jesus out for thirty pieces of silver. Disciples should never become thieves. God is Jehovah-Jireh. He will provide for you. Judas Iscariot's insight was skewed because Satan entered him. Remember Satan will use those who allow themselves to be used. There were signs that Judas Iscariot was mistaken in his ability to see and understand the nature of Jesus Christ. When Mary took the ointment and anointed the feet of Jesus, it was Judas Iscariot who asked why she didn't sale the ointment and give it to the poor. Go beyond rituals, traditions, and thievery. Release it now by the power of Jesus Christ!

Insight that is not given to spiritual understanding from the Lord God, leads to separation. Ownership of attachments of addictions, bad habits, and quick tempers begins to form. A person is now under the guise that they are the monster they themselves created. Not so.

Allow your mind to be turned back to God. Begin to claim what He claims for your life. How long will you state, "I AM a recovering"? Once God cleans you up, you are no longer to claim what society deems as a lifelong problem that will occur. He will show you who you are in Him. It is up to you to believe Christ when He shows you, you. You did not wake up in addiction, rude behaviors, or ill-manners.

There were evil, negative seeds planted in your life. They took time to form and so must your transformation to God. If you believe, then pray and ask God to help your unbelief. Saul of the New Testament was attached to his religious beliefs. He was the son of a Pharisee and was educated in Orthodox Judaism. He was a brilliant student. When he was older, he began persecuting men and women who were of "The Way" based on his attachment. Jesus intervened, asked a question, and so the conversion of Saul to Paul began. Paul relinquished his attachment to religion and embraced or attached himself to Jesus Christ. He went on attached in Jesus' name evangelizing. He endured stoning, beatings because his attachment to the Source of sources far outweighed what man could do to him. Attach yourself to Jesus Christ. Be converted by the renewing of your mind.

Godly Release

Now, for those who are bold enough to take God at His word, you can change in an instant. Cut out everyone, everything, and every place that is not of God. Find a Bible based church that will feed you proper nutrients from God. Pray much as well as read and study God's word. Start right now. Change your number if you have to. Do whatever it takes NOW. Pour out the liquor. Flush the illegal substances. Do whatever it takes NOW. Seek Godly counsel to help you focus on the things of God. You can be set free right NOW. God is waiting on you. He can release you from the hands of the enemy. He is Jehovah-Mephalti. He is your deliverer. He is Jehovah-Rapha. He is your healer. He is Omnipotent. God is all powerful.

Father God in the awesome name of Jesus Christ, thank You for the release that I am now experiencing. Thank You Lord God for showing me ways to release unto You Lord God, that I may submit and yield unto You God. Father continue to release those things from me that I develop the proper attachment to You Jesus creating a Holy and Righteous stronghold. I am in a posture of thanksgiving unto You Jesus. Thank You Holy Spirit for purging and filling me. Thank You Lord for sending me hope when I felt all was lost. Thank You Jesus for another chance to renew my mind. Lord I will not stop renewing my mind with Your knowledge, wisdom, and understanding. I will not stop seeking out righteous strongholds in You Lord. Spirit of the Living God, continue to teach me Your precepts, commands, and statutes. I thank You Lord for allowing me to see You moving in my life. Thank You Jesus for encamping Your host of angels around me protecting me from hurt, harm, and danger. Thank You Lord God for Your grace and mercy. Continue to allow Your Word to work in me, on me, and through me. I desire to go further and higher in You Jesus. I declare and decree that my life is changed in You Lord. I declare and decree the release has taken place by Your precious anointing Lord God. By Your precious blood Jesus, I will never be the same. No more of me Lord, but all of You Jesus. God I lay prostrate before You. Holy Spirit I willing decrease that You may increase in me. This is Your servant's prayer. Amen.

If you do not feel that you can stop right this moment but need a step down program this is completely acceptable. The main point is to return to God. If you start that is a step. God honors sincerity, just keep on stepping. I heard a preacher state that the first thirty days of forming a new mind set or changing was "discipline." In order to be converted you have to submit to Godly regulations. The next thirty days is stated to be "habit." Yielding to Godly regulations generates Godly patterns. The following thirty days is a changed "lifestyle." You will more easily live a life unto God and all of His righteousness, striving to be more like your Creator. It takes ninety days of yielding to God in order to vindicate a Godly mind set. This does not mean that you stop pursuing God. It means that your spiritual connection of going after God becomes easier to do in spite of any trials, tribulations, or obstacles that will rise.

When stumbling blocks, attacks by the enemy, misuse by family members, and friends stab you in the back, you will be able to shake the dust from your clothes because your focus is on Jesus Christ being the head of your life. The more you follow Jesus Christ, the more you will expand your mind to the mind of God. Press forward in Christ and receive your just reward. God is Jehovah-M'Kaddesh. He is the Lord who sanctifies. Allow Christ to make you whole and set you apart for His service.

Remember that Satan can only imitate God because he wants to be God. Satan is conniving. He leads people to believe that slipups and acting outside of God's Will is acceptable. But God is lifting up a standard. God is sounding the alarm for His people to be restored to walking in authority and power over the enemy.

Chapter 9

The Stronghold of God

Return to your stronghold, O prisoners of hope; today I declare that I will restore to you double. For I have bent Judah as my bow; I have made Ephraim its arrow. I will arouse your sons, O Zion, against your sons, O Greece, and wield you like a warrior's sword. Then the Lord will appear over them, and his arrow go forth like lightning; the Lord God will sound the trumpet and march forth in the whirlwinds of the south. The Lord of hosts will protect them, and they shall devour and tread down the slingers; they shall drink their blood like wine, and be full like a bowl, drenched like the corners of the altar. On that day the Lord their God will save them for they are the flock of his people; for like the jewels of a crown they shall shine on his land. For what goodness and beauty are his! Grain shall make the young men flourish, and new wine the young women. Zechariah 9:12-17 ESV

There are so many liberties in God. However, the enemy only wants you to focus and concentrate on the restrictions. By keeping your focus on the restrictions you lose sight that the Scripture passage states whom the Son sets free is free indeed. God only places restrictions or forbids those things that will harm you; those things that will cause you to die in sin and spend eternity in hell.

As you release, restoration of the heart, body, soul, and spirit are in order. The spirit will be discussed in the last chapter of this book. It is there you will discover the Ta'mar Spirit. But, first you must understand what the heart, body, and soul are according to Scripture in order to fully engage the stronghold of the Lord.

Heart

And Noah builded an altar unto the LORD; and took of every clean beast, and of every clean fowl, and offered burnt offerings on the altar. And the LORD smelled a sweet savor; and the LORD said in his heart, I will not again curse the ground any more for man's sake; for the imagination of man's heart is evil from his youth; neither

119

will I again smite any more every thing living, as I have done. While the earth remaineth, seedtime and harvest, and cold and heat, and summer and winter, and day and night shall not cease. *Genesis 8:20-22 KJV*

The heart is the innermost being. Your heart is the arena for Divine influence. The heart and emotions are often tied together in description. Your heart is what will respond to God. The heart is also a physical organ that pumps blood throughout the body. If the heart stops, life ceases to exist. Your heart physically and spiritually is vital to your walk with God. Your heart will convict you when your mind will ignore the conviction. The heart will have empathy whereas your mind will have apathy.

Ref: Acts 15:6-11

Body

I beseech you therefore, brethren, by the mercies of God, that ye present your bodies a living sacrifice, Holy, acceptable unto God, which is your reasonable service. And be not conformed to this world: but be ye transformed by the renewing of your mind, that ye may prove what is that good, and acceptable, and perfect, will of God. For I say, through the grace given unto me, to every man that is among you, not to think of himself more highly than he ought to think; but to think soberly, according as God hath dealt to every man the measure of faith. *Romans 12:1-3 KJV*

Your body is the physical temple or ark that houses your soul/spirit. Once the Holy Spirit has come upon you, you should be careful not to misuse and abuse your temple. Spiritually speaking, you become part of the body of Christ. You are an individual member. When you defile your body (temple/ark), it is like the body of Christ has an infection. This is why the Scriptures state to present your body as a living sacrifice. You are now a vital component to the body. You must sacrifice your will for the Will of the Father. Jesus Christ knows what is best for the Body. He is the Head. Allow Him to reign and rule.

Ref: Matthew 6:21-24

Soul

And the LORD God formed man of the dust of the ground, and breathed into his nostrils the breath of life; and man became a living soul. *Genesis 2:7 KJV*

The soul is the seat of your ego. The soul is considered the "self." Your soul is a triune consisting of your mind, will, and emotions. Your soul and spirit man are always at war with each other. Your spirit is cultivated by spiritual nourishment. Your soul is swayed by physical sensations. To completely understand the soul, you must look at the mind, will, and emotions separately.

Mind

That ye put off concerning the former conversation the old man, which is corrupt according to the deceitful lusts; And be renewed in the spirit of your mind; And that ye put on the new man, which after God is created in righteousness and true holiness. *Ephesians 4:22-24 KJV*

Ephesians states "be renewed in the **spirit** of your mind." The spirit in this instance deals with the invisible, powerful authority of the triune God. Your mind is the reflective awareness. Your mind contains your perception of how things are viewed and understood. Based on your conclusion to a matter, you feel, judge, and determine accordingly. If your mind has been not been renewed by the spirit, the Holy Ghost, then you are drawing inaccurate conclusions. You are judging according to the world and not according to God. You must take the time to retrain your mind through the Spirit of God.

Ref: Philippians 2:5

Will

After this manner therefore pray ye: Our Father which art in heaven, Hallowed be thy name. Thy kingdom come. Thy will be done in earth, as it is in heaven. Give us this day our daily bread. And forgive us our debts,

as we forgive our debtors. And lead us not into temptation, but deliver us from evil: For thine is the kingdom, and the power, and the glory, for ever. Amen. For if ye forgive men their trespasses, your heavenly Father will also forgive you: But if ye forgive not men their trespasses, neither will your Father forgive your trespasses. *Matthew 6:9-15 KJV*

The will is your choice, inclination, pleasure, or desire within the soul. Your will unless changed, shall conflict with the Will of God. God's Will is for the soul to obey His commands and precepts. So the will is the freedom of choice. God does not inflict His Will upon you. You have to forsake your will and do the Will of the Father. People who state they have no will power are mistaken. It is your will that is powering you to desire whatever you are craving. By stating you have no will power means you do not have a choice in what your body does. That is a dangerous place to be both in the positive and negative. Positive if you have no will power of your own but are allowing God's Will to be done in your life. You do not want to stray from the presence of God, so you do not have the will power to leave His presence. Negative if you have no will, or choice, or desire to want to be in the presence of God.

Ref: Psalms 143:7-12

Emotions

That they should seek the Lord, if haply they might feel after him, and find him, though he be not far from every one of us: For in him we live, and move, and have our being; as certain also of your own poets have said, For we are also his offspring. Forasmuch then as we are the offspring of God, we ought not to think that the Godhead is like unto gold, or silver, or stone, graven by art and man's device. *Acts 17:27-29 KJV*

The terminology "emotions" is not expressly used in the Bible. However, the usage of words such as joy, grief, anger, sorrow, weeping, fear which are used, are all various types of emotions. Your emotions are therefore, outward expressions of inward feelings. Emotions are either healthy or unhealthy. Healthy emotions are tied to reverencing, worshipping, and pleasing God. Unhealthy emotions are living worldly, which are tied to the Prince of Persia. The enemy does not mind you going to church if your emotions are still skewed.

Ref: Psalms 103:13-18

The Word of the Lord is the tiller of the soil of your mind. Through the pages of this book, the Holy Spirit has been working, turning over the ground of your mind. Weeds have been removed and nutrients rich in newness of life have been added to ensure healthy growth. The Sower has taken a survey, counted up the cost, and decided the timing was right to begin sowing into your life. As He moves, some seed falls by the way side, some on stony ground, some among thorns, but the other on good ground. You are good ground! The journey has not been about just "another good read" but it has been about becoming fertile ground for the Lord. God desires that you yield His fruit which will spring up and increase. The Sower is also the Source of growth. He is the True Vine. Realize that you are His branch. Abiding in Jesus enables you to bear productive, spiritual fruit.

There is a lot that needs to be taken to the threshing floor in order to prepare the spirit. Continue to surrender to God, lying before Him so that all the chaff in your life may be blown away. God desires the grain of you. He wants to water you so that you grow in Him. He wants you to produce from Him. The Ta'mar Spirit will show just how the storms of your life will cause you to produce for God. Weeping may endure for a night but joy does come in the morning. The joy of the Lord is your strength, therefore, be strong and of good courage.

The Spirit of God

> And there shall come forth a rod out of the stem of Jesse, and a Branch shall grow out of his roots: And the spirit of the LORD shall rest upon him, the spirit of wisdom and understanding, the spirit of counsel and might, the spirit of knowledge and of the fear of the LORD; And shall make him of quick understanding in the fear of the LORD: and he shall not judge after the sight of his eyes, neither reprove after the hearing of his ears: But with

righteousness shall he judge the poor, and reprove with equity for the meek of the earth: and he shall smite the earth with the rod of his mouth, and with the breath of his lips shall he slay the wicked. And righteousness shall be the girdle of his loins, and faithfulness the girdle of his reins. The wolf also shall dwell with the lamb, and the leopard shall lie down with the kid; and the calf and the young lion and the fatling together; and a little child shall lead them. And the cow and the bear shall feed; their young ones shall lie down together: and the lion shall eat straw like the ox. And the sucking child shall play on the hole of the asp, and the weaned child shall put his hand on the cockatrice' den. They shall not hurt nor destroy in all my Holy mountain: for the earth shall be full of the knowledge of the LORD, as the waters cover the sea. *Isaiah 11:1-9 KJV*

It is imperative that you grow to fully grasp the sevenfold Spirit of God. You must understand that God and Jesus Christ are One in Perfect and Complete harmony. There is no separation from perfect completeness; being whole in the Lord. Knowing this means that you are also perfectly whole and complete.

Get a handle of the Spirit of the Lord. This Spirit is a supernatural power that creates God's thoughts in your heart. When Jesus was baptized, He immediately saw the heavens open up. The Spirit of God came down like a dove and rested on Him. This is what baptisms are purposed for. Not to just get wet, dry off, and live the same sinful life. You must be born again in order to see the Kingdom of God.

The Spirit of Wisdom is next. The Spirit is all of God's thoughts. The Lord will place all of His laws in your mind. He will write them in your heart. When He does this He becomes God in your life and you become part of His people. He becomes your Lord. God will rule your life. The Bibles states that through wisdom a house is built. You must understand how to build your temple unto the Lord.

The Spirit of Understanding follows. God will personally illuminate His thoughts to you. Understand that a house is established by understanding. Ask God to make you understand

His precepts that you may speak of His wonderful works. Glory is always returned to the Father.

The Spirit of Counsel and Might is the next step. It deals with God's personal instructions for Godly choices. God is a wonderful counselor. He is well qualified to give suitable and proper advice. Seeking His counsel empowers you to run this race.

The Spirit of Strength is the next part. It concerns God's supernatural ability to perform those thoughts in your life. God is a God who thinks, speaks, and manifests things into existence. The Lord exercises love and kindness towards you. Seeking Him first and all His righteousness will cause Him to move and manifest blessings on your behalf. God works in you, to will and to do His good pleasure. There is nothing done of your own accord while operating in the Lord. You are strengthened in Christ to do all things.

The Spirit of Knowledge is the next piece. See God's thoughts being manifested in your life actions. By knowledge you are able to fill the chambers of your house with ALL precious and pleasant riches. People are destroyed for a lack of knowledge. Christ was crucified and you are, subsequently crucified with Him. He is now in you by the Holy Spirit. The Holy Spirit will give you Holy and Righteous knowledge so that you are not destroyed.

The Fear of the Lord is the final step. Walk in God's love and truth. Resist all things that would quench His Spirit. Reverence the Lord. Closely adhere to His Will being done. Do what pleases God not man. When you fear the Lord, He will hear you when you cry out to Him. He will move and assign warring angels to keep you lest you dash your foot against a stone.

Chapter 10

The Ta'mar Spirit

And Ta'mar put ashes on her head, and rent her garment of divers colours that was on her, and laid her hand on her head, and went on crying. And Ab'salom her brother said unto her, Hath Am'non thy brother been with thee? but hold now thy peace, my sister: he is thy brother; regard not this thing. So Ta'mar remained desolate in her brother Ab'salom's house. II Samuel 13:19, 20

The Bible from the dawn of time as always been accepted within the Christian church. It is viewed as the revelation of God. The Bible contains a measure of standards and norms every faith walker follows. It is God's spoken Truth.

The Bible is whole and complete. Nothing is to be taken from it and nothing should be added to it. Always believe the report of the Lord. He is Alpha and Omega. He is the Author and Finisher of your course.

It is time to allow the Holy Spirit to finish establishing the Ta'mar Spirit within you. Press beyond the mundane to get to the mark of a higher calling in Christ Jesus. God does not want you in a permanent bent out of shape position. He wants you to stand and be erect before, during, and after storms.

Ta'mar in the Bible is about realizing your worth in Christ. You are a handsome man of God. You are a beautiful woman of God. The enemy has seen your splendor and has set a course to destroy you. However, because the Holy Spirit dwells within you it cannot happen. The Spirit of the living God sustains you. The Ta'mar Spirit is the Spirit of Peace. The tempest may rise against you but the Peace of God will keep you going.

Heavenly Father, in the name of Jesus I come with a bowed head and humbled heart. Lord I repent and turn from sinful, wicked ways. Jesus I will trust You before

and after storms. Lord God I am ready, willing, and now able to stand firm on the promises You gave. I am standing on Your Word. Father I reject all manner of evil influence. Lord I desire to live for and please You. Jesus I now say not my will but Thy will be done in my life. I declare and decree that I am no more my own but I realize that I have been bought with a price. Thank You Jesus for paying the price for me. I look to You Father for counsel, guidance, and instructions. Lord God I will seek out and study Your Word for every test and temptation that is presented to me. Lord God help me to know Your Truth. I ask and thank You Jesus for answering my prayers. Amen.

There is something about the Peace of God. His Peace gives comfort. This comfort surpasses all understanding. When you have God's Peace, you are not easily rattled or shaken. You trust that God is working on your behalf.

Just before II Samuel 13, we find Da'vid repenting for his indiscretion. If you read II Samuel chapters 11 and 12 as instructed from Chapter 2, you know exactly why Da'vid was asking for forgiveness from the Lord. Make the connection that there is always divine purpose and reason for Godly instructions. At times you may not understand why instructions are given but divine instructions should always be followed. If you still have not read these chapters, I admonish you to do so now.

It was only after the Lord sent Nathan, that Da'vid realized the depths of his sins. Shortly thereafter, the King pens Psalm 51, which is a prayer of repentance. At the end of the prayer, Da'vid stated he would still praise the Lord. Da'vid understood God required true repentance through a broken spirit and contrite heart. Da'vid trusted that God would not despise these types of sacrifices. Da'vid sinned and, yet, he continued to trust in God. Da'vid mourned for his sick child, the one conceived in sin. But, he was at peace when the child passed. Da'vid rose from the ground, washed and anointed himself, changed his garments, and immediately went into the house of the Lord to worship. This is the peace that his servants did not understand. Da'vid did not linger in the state of mourning over his transgressions and its consequences. He was at peace.

This is exactly the final posture of Ta'mar. "The Father is Peace" invited her to stay in his house. It is there within the house where Ta'mar remained in a desolate stance; not worrying about people talking and spreading rumors about what happened. Ta'mar remained in the House of Peace. This is what God wants you to do. He does not want you to relive the nightmare of your past haunts. He wants you to remain in Him. He wants you to live in peace. Once this is accomplished then you can spread a personal testimony about your past, so that others may also be released from bondage. You can be a ray of hope for them. Develop a, "If I can make it so can you," attitude in Christ Jesus. It is easy when you have tried Him and know Him to be faithful.

We have all experienced traumatic episodes in our lives. From living in single parent homes, to molestation and abuse, to experiments with drugs and alcohol but God is Jehovah-shalom. He is the God of Peace. God is Jehovah Rophe. He is the Lord who heals. The Lord is also El Shaddai. He is God Almighty.

> Let God arise, let his enemies be scattered: let them also that hate him flee before him. As smoke is driven away, so drive them away: as wax melteth before the fire, so let the wicked perish at the presence of God. But let the righteous be glad; let them rejoice before God: yea, let them exceedingly rejoice. Sing unto God, sing praises to his name: extol him that rideth upon the heavens by his name JAH, and rejoice before him. A father of the fatherless, and a judge of the widows, is God in his Holy habitation. God setteth the solitary in families: he bringeth out those which are bound with chains: but the rebellious dwell in a dry land. *Psalm 68:1-6 KJV*

Now that God has arisen in your life, let His enemies be scattered. You are not your storm, but with Jesus Christ you are a force to be reckoned with.

A famous singer once said, "Everything you go through is so because it makes you the best you, you can be. What you experience molds you. Your story might not be exactly the same as someone else's story but there may be a connection made. That

129

person going through will connect with the story and see that there is glory waiting in store for going through."

Again I say, you are not your storm. You are a force to be reckoned with. Jesus is the surge, the very essence of energy that churns within. Do not glorify the areas where you fall short. Love yourself where you are while glorifying God for where you are headed. Never become complacent in God. There are always new levels, new dimensions, and new realms to be discovered.

> **"Whatever you compromise to keep is what you lose. Whatever you compromise to give is what you keep."** ~ **Author unknown**

So where do you begin; ground zero. You begin in your heart. Realize that you do not have to take on your sins, sickness because Jesus bore many stripes on my and your behalf. He wore a crown of thorns that marked Him. He took on corruptible because He is incorruptible. He took on all those things that you and I could not handle because He loves us that much. Jesus was obedient even unto death. So take off the façade of "I can handle it." The reality is that you cannot, otherwise you would be serving God in ALL the beauty of Holiness.

You do not have to be strong in your own strength. Your strength is fleeting. All you need is joy in the Lord. The Bible declares that the joy of the Lord is your strength. Now this is true strength.

Ref: Matthew 5:3-12

Starting Point

The Ta'mar Spirit can be ignited within; you have to know all that Ta'mar means. **Ta'mar** means "date palm." Date palms are commonly known as Palm Trees. **Ta'mar**, from an unused root, means "to be erect; a palm tree." Palm Trees stand erect during storms. They have high wind-resistant foliage. They are less prone to toppling in wind storms. Palms can also flourish in any type of climate or condition. There are between 2500 to 3000 species of palms.

Where did palms get their start? Palms are very unique and hard to confuse with any other plant. Palms are speculated to have originated in Mesopotamia over 6,000 years ago. The palm is also mentioned in the Bible several times. The Date Palm is known as the Phoenix dactylifera of Linnaeus. It reaches heights of forty to eighty feet. Light is a key element in palm growth. Palms can also survive in complete darkness for a sizeable period of time. Water is another key element to growth. But most palms are tolerant of dry places.

After a palm is first planted it takes about six to eight years to bear fruit. Thereafter, it bears fruit for about a century. The fruit is called **drupe**. It is defined as a "fleshy, one-seeded fruit with a thick and sclerotic endocarp that does not open or split at maturity." The fruit and seed are rich in fat, including oil and wax. The trunk is straight, tall, and unbroken. The trunk is made up of old leaves. This is known as leaf scars. The top of the palm adorns gigantic leaves that could reach twenty feet.

The fruit is a daily staple for some cultures. Its sap also furnishes wine. The fibers at the base of the leaves are used to make rope and leaves are constructed to make brushes, mats, bags, couches, and baskets. Palm leaves are called blades and depending on the species of palm, leaves are either fan, or bifid shaped. These leaves are also known as the crown of the palm. Truly the palm supplies just about all of a person's needs.

Here is a list of some references of palms in the Bible:

- **Exodus 15:27**
- **Jericho was the city of "palm trees." Deuteronomy 34:3**
- **Eze'ki-el 41:19**
- **Genesis 38:6**

Palms are not trees. A **Tree** is a "large, woody perennial plant with one main trunk and many branches. A **Branch** is "any woody extension from a tree or shrub; limb." Palms do not have branches.

Palms are classified as monocots. Monocots are flowering plants. Examples of other monocots are lilies, grass, irises, and orchids to name a few. Palms have more in common in their structure and processes with lawn grasses, corn, and rice than oak or maple trees and roses. Very few monocots grow as large as palms. Palm roots grow laterally. Their growth links them to their parent palm sometimes over one hundred feet away.

Based on the very broad description given above, palms are very versatile and elusive. For all of the research that has been done on these monocots, scientists are still baffled by the palms. This has spiritual significance. You cannot use science to figure God out. He said in His Word that you and I would flourish like the palm trees. Intellect cannot be used to determine the whole of something so spiritual.

The world will try to figure you out. It will try to use its experience to determine how you are able to thrive. But God will take the simple things to perplex those who profess to be wise. The world will be dumbfounded to see you growing in seemingly dry and desert places. The world will witness you bearing fruit. The world will also be an eyewitness to you in your storm and yet you will still be standing after the storm has subsided. This is how God operates. It is not for you to be glorified. It is all done so that He may be glorified. The very mystery of the palm will cause onlookers to become curious. Those who are not saved will be saved because you flourished through God. The backsliders will return to God because you have become an example by your testimony. God is faithful and just.

Destined to Flourish

The righteous shall flourish like the palm tree: he shall grow like a cedar in Lebanon. Those that be planted in the house of the LORD shall flourish in the courts of our God. They shall still bring forth fruit in old age; they

shall be fat and flourishing; To show that the LORD is upright: he is my rock, and there is no unrighteousness in him. *Psalm 92:12-15 KJV*

This Psalm was written in conjunction with the book of Nehemiah. In Nehemiah 13, we find the prophet instructing the children of Is'rael who were in Jeru'salem on the principles of separation. **Jeru'salem** means "the habitation of peace." The enemy by way of To'biah was attempting to infiltrate a Holy nation to wipe out its peace. The physical temple had been destroyed. Nehemiah was charged with getting the people to worship God as well as observe the Sabbath beyond the present physical restraints. Though Nehemiah was severe in his enforcement, he understood worship as vital to peace. Worship was to be spiritual not physical. True worship was to be done unto God and not for the sake of religious mechanics.

Religion keeps a person mourning at the Cross. Worship moves you pass the Cross on a quest to seek after the Will of God. It is time to move beyond the Cross. You were saved when Jesus Christ went to the Cross. But, there is more to the story. You are now a Christian. A **Christian** is a "follower of Christ." You must adhere to Christ. Your name is no longer important. Do not seek after vain glory.

Ref: *I Peter 4:12-19*

Being a Christian is important because this is the first step in understanding Christ. A Christian suffers for righteousness' sake. Jesus Christ is accepted and this is instrumental to being Christ like. Followers of Christ walk according to His Holy footsteps. Believers of Christ witness healings and miracles that the world regards as a hoax. Christians exercise patience on their faith walk with Christ. Christians spend lifetimes coming into the full knowledge and understanding of who Christ is and who they are in Him. Subsequently, Christians are longsuffering, enduring all things. Sin is ever present but the elect of God choose to operate in the Spirit of God which is peaceful at all times.

Possess the fruits of the spirit because of the mark of Christ on you. Generate fruit in love, joy, peace, longsuffering, gentleness, goodness, faith, meekness, and temperance. As children of Christ, crucify the flesh so that the affections and lusts are not fulfilled thereof. You must die daily. Check daily to ensure the right kind of fruit is being produced for others to partake of. This type of fruit is empowering. Comprehend the importance of the fruit in that it draws people to Christ. This Spiritual Fruit is lasting; it does not have an expiration date. This fruit does not spoil or rot. This Spiritual Fruit is eternal because it comes from God the Father.

Know that God is with you because He is in you through the Holy Spirit. As a Christian, you have to have a willingness to endure for the long haul because Christ endured. He is your Godly example. Emulate Christ. Do unto others as you would have them do unto you. Do not seek revenge, as Christ did not settle the score when you were of the world and persecuted Him by walking in unbelief and disobedience. As a Christian, be good because God is good. He sent His only begotten Son so that you may not perish but have everlasting life. Rely and hope on the things not seen because they are manifested from the invisible, spiritual realm of God. Therefore, your faith is the key to bringing the invisible to the visible. As a Christian, do not force your beliefs in Christ on anyone. Simply live a Godly lifestyle so that Christ is seen in and through you. Lift up Christ and He will draw all men unto Him.

Ref: I Peter 4:16

Once you come into the revelatory knowledge of a Christian, move further into Christ. Take the role as a Christian one step further. Become an ambassador for Christ. Christian is mentioned twice in the Bible while Ambassador is mentioned four times. **Ambassador** means "to be older, prior by birth or in age." Another meaning of **ambassador** is "a diplomatic official of the highest rank, sent by one sovereign or state to another as its resident representative; or an authorized messenger or representative." Become more than a follower of Christ, become a messenger for Christ.

Ref: Ephesians 6:10-20

Be adherent to Christ and an ambassador to the world; starting with your local community. Begin in your home representing Christ, then branch out. The Bible is God's spoken Word. God spoke it and that settles it. Just think of the palm, its flexibility, and its determined growth, even when loaded with weights astonishes those who do not believe. But God said that you would prosper. You are of "The Way" because God said that He was the Way, the Truth, and the Life. Represent the Kingdom of God. You are only a sojourner on the earth. While here, you are God's elected representative who has the authority and dominion to act on God's behalf.

Be it flood, whirlwind, hurricane, squall, blizzard, you were placed on this earth to show others how to endure. Rise Spirit of Ta'mar! You have been endowed with the authority and power to stand erect like the palm. You are erect because of the understanding of the mind of Christ as well as the statutes and precepts of God. You know what you know in Christ and you understand it is God who knows all. Because He knows all, commit to fully understanding all that He gives in knowledge, wisdom, and understanding.

One unique feature of the palm is that there are no rings to determine its age. Therefore, without physically watching a palm, one would not know the age of a palm. When you decide to serve God in spirit and truth you tap into infinite, eternality. God is ageless. People will marvel at the wisdom and knowledge you possess in Christ Jesus. The God you serve is from everlasting to everlasting.

In moving beyond the Cross realize the momentous undertaking an ambassador must accept. You must have faith that exceeds the world's understanding. Know that faith is the substance of things hoped for and the evidence of things not seen. Therefore, operate in the spiritual realm which is invisible to the carnal eye. Do not become easily affected by the questions the enemy asks because the answers come from the Bible, which is divinely inspired by God. When Jesus was tempted by the devil the Word says that Jesus answered according to what God said. Jesus fought by the power

135

of God and not in his own strength in the flesh. You have to know what "is written" in the Word of God. Do not justify yourself to the world. You have been justified in Christ.

Ambassadors always adorn the whole armor of God; they never take the armor off. Be in tuned with the Holy Spirit continuously. Go beyond the Cross to the battlefield. Stand on the battlefield while God uses you to show His enemies He is Jehovah-Sabaoth. He is the Lord of Hosts. As the Body of Christ, we are His hosts. You are part of His army. As an ambassador, always be ready to represent God. Move beyond the Cross because of the knowledge that you do not fight against flesh and blood. You are in spiritual warfare, fighting against principalities in high places. How should you fight against these principalities? Implement God's Word. His Word is the only way to defeat the enemy. Do not attempt to battle spiritual wickedness in the flesh. As an ambassador, you recognize that there is no good thing that dwells in the flesh.

Christ was rejected by the world and, therefore, we do not expect to be accepted either. The Holy Spirit was given as a Comforter while Jesus Christ is absent. Hence, operate under the directive of the Holy Spirit. You have to constantly deprogram the spirit of your mind from the things of this world. Habitually program your mind to allow the Holy Spirit to be your navigator. The Holy Spirit will lead you in all truth. Satan has no hold because you keep the Truth of God within. Pray constantly, study the Word, fast, and tap into the spiritual realm for guidance in all truth. The whole armor of God is for offence and defense. With this knowledge and understanding of the whole armor of God, boldly hold your head up. Dwell in immoral places no longer. Have confidence in God.

You have moved beyond the Cross to accept your calling in Christ Jesus. Strive to be the best; serving in the spirit of excellence. Upon walking in the call of Christ, be watchful and diligent about your Father's business. God has entrusted you to spread the Gospel. Your calling leads to further advancement of the Kingdom of God. Like the military, infiltrate dry and desolate places conquering and converting lost souls that are destined for hell. Through the authority and power of the Commander-in-Chief, souls are won to Christ. This is never done by your own power but by the power of God. Become His mouthpiece. For Christ, be His light that shines here on earth. Understand your position and calling. Get training. You are charged to set up Holy embassies all over this world for Christ. Think globally but start locally.

An ambassador should have great courage. Though you may not be imprisoned for spreading the Gospel as in the days of the Bible, you may, however, be wearied by the world's attempt to shut you up. Let's link together spiritually by continuous prayer for one another. In moving beyond the Cross, know that you represent a portion of the Body of Christ. Bear the burden of your fellow laborers in the Gospel. Strengthen and encourage one another. Do not degrade anyone. There are many members but one body in Christ. Therefore, be the catalyst for making sure that the body operates as a whole.

Become a Palm Ambassador presenting your body as a living sacrifice. Palm branches are symbolic of victory and peace.

Move according to the Holy Spirit without question. Obedience is better than sacrifice. As an ambassador, do the work that the world says is unorthodox. This is how to flourish. Someone somewhere is waiting on a sign from God. As an ambassador, follow directions because you are delivering Godly answers to people on the verge of yielding to Jesus Christ as the Lord and Saviour of their lives. Become a sower, planting the seed of Jesus Christ in people's lives. Move beyond the Cross because you know Christ still lives.

Moving beyond the Cross exacts greater works. In accomplishing the Will of the Father you are bound to flourish.

Ref: John 14:12-18

Believers in Christ, operate in Him asking that things to be done in His name because Jesus Christ has all power. He said in His Word that He would do it; accomplish greater works through Him. As an ambassador, walk with Him in the Spirit. Believe on Him through the Holy Spirit. It is because of your belief that you should move beyond the Cross into greater works.

There are greater opportunities to perform miraculous works because Jesus Christ returned to His Father. Christ is your intercessor. Achieve greater works because it is not your will in which you are seeking to fulfill. You seek to fulfill the Will of God the Father. You must decrease that the Lord be increased in you. According to your measure of faith, accomplish the mission Christ has imparted to you.

Part of the Fixture

> And their windows, and their arches, and their palm trees, were after the measure of the gate that looketh toward the east; and they went up unto it by seven steps; and the arches thereof were before them. And the gate of the inner court was over against the gate toward the north, and toward the east; and he measured from gate to gate an hundred cubits. After that he brought me toward the south, and behold a gate toward the south: and he measured the posts thereof and the arches thereof according to these measures. And there were windows in it and in the arches thereof round about, like those windows: the length was fifty cubits, and the breadth five and twenty cubits. And there were seven steps to go up to it, and the arches thereof were before them: and it had palm trees, one on this side, and another on that side, upon the posts thereof. *Eze'ki-el 40:22-26 KJV*

Now that you have decided to move beyond the Cross, thrive because you represent righteousness. Do what is right; abide by the laws of God. You are vindicated by God. You should now become a law abiding citizen in the Kingdom of God.

Righteousness allows you to become part of God's temple in Is'rael. **Is'rael** means "the prince who prevails with God." This is significant because the Word calls you royal. As royalty you are allowed access to the King. You are a gatekeeper for God's house; His Holy temple. In the previous Scriptures, the wall surrounding the temple was measured. This signifies the separation of the church from the world. Because you are a post leading to the temple, you are already separated from the world. Become a permanent fixture in the safety of the Lord's house like Ta'mar. Let peace be your dwelling place. Be in a posture of constant fellowship with the Lord. He made the post that is now you.

God can and will completely break you of the worldly habits – releasing and purging your of all negative strongholds. His Omnipotence can pull you out of the muck and mire. He is the God of the impossible. Allow the Holy Spirit to purge you of the world and worldly ways. Become soft and pliable; the Lord can begin to mold and shape you according to His Will – releasing the Holy Spirit to establish Godly strongholds. He will breathe new life into you and cause you to grow as a palm tree. Your spirit can be quickened and you will begin to stand erect in God. Become a post in Christ which is unmovable even during the storm.

The posts mentioned in the Scripture were tall like palm trees. Astonish the world by spiritually standing tall and flourishing. If you are positioned in places with outrageous heat, flourish even in the heat. Flourish in the flood. Flourish! Flourish in affliction because God has crafted you to do so. Understand that you are to endure all types of evil and wickedness. You already have the victory.

You are a palm! In the ancient times, the winners of events were bestowed with palms. But, you are not bestowed with a palm. The enemy would try to snatch your victory away. Or, you may drop your palm. Therefore, God made you into a palm. He made you into victory. You are an everlasting palm. You are engraved on the posts of the temple. Therefore, honor God because you are part of His temple just like Ta'mar remained in the Father's House in Peace.

Notice there are seven steps leading up to the temple. Seven is the number of perfection or completion. You are a complete and perfect palm fixture in God. You are His ornament leading to His temple. You are perfect in the beauty of God's Holiness that draws people to come closer and take a look on the inside.

Ref: I Corinthians 15:57, 58

You should become unmovable. Do not allow the world to move you to sin against God any more. Concerning the matters of God; be steadfast. The storms are worth enduring so that you continue to abound in the Lord. No longer shall you throw immature temper tantrums because the Lord has matured you. Do not tolerate or allow evil to infiltrate your temple be it in fellowship with one another or your physical temple where the Holy Spirit dwells. You have the authority to cast out evil in the name of Jesus. Do not run from evil but be unmovable by using the Word of God to combat the enemy.

Be sound in Godly principles and practice what you preach. The purpose for which Christ has called you is mighty. Operate according to your calling in season and out of season. Do not be moved from your calling. God has appointed you to your position. God through Christ Jesus qualified you and you should not be moved. Your testimonies bring salvation for lost souls by the power of Christ that lives in you. You are now well equipped and weighted with the Word of God.

Fleshly desires should no longer move you. Be moved only when God tells you to move. When the Holy Spirit gently whispers instructions on moving, know that it is divine. Navigate through life according to the succession of God and not man. If God does not instruct you to move be steadfast in your position. People may not understand your obstinacies. They do not have to. Follow the leading of Jesus Christ.

Convert sinners by being a post of God. Sinners should not be able to convert you to the world or to Satan. Do not worship the things of Satan. He has no place in your life. Seeking God and resisting the enemy causes the devil to flee. Edify the saints of God because you are His fixed post. Exemplify your likeness as a palm which goes through but still remains in peace, love, and joy. Wave your hands and cry aloud with rejoicing unto God like the leaves of a palm. Your flesh may be encountering attacks but you serve a higher power. Once you tap into God, you have instant victory regardless of what situations may "look" like. Stand steadfast in God. Like a palm tree stretches and grows, so will God stretch out in you as you stretch out in Him.

In holding fast to your profession that Jesus Christ is your Chief Priest, you are not enduring in vain. Therefore, do not store up treasures on earth. Your treasures lie in heaven. When the world tries to tempt you with earthly possessions do not be moved. These worldly possessions will corrode and are corrupt. Do not receive rust and shadiness from the world. However, receive the riches. The wealth of the wicked is stored up for the righteous. Your faith is strong. Do not turn aside from serving the Lord.

Understand that being steadfast, unmovable, and always abounding is threefold. A threefold cord is not easily broken so says the Lord. Therefore, be not easily swayed from your stance.

The Word of God is the living truth; because you believe the truth you will not be shaken or stagger by false information, false teachers, and the like. You shall stand erect like a palm. You are immovable in your expectation that you shall be caught up with Jesus. You will put on incorruptible with Him. Knowing this, you shall not renounce nor resign from your post. God's foundation is sure. You are connected to God like palms are connected to their parent palm. Your hope should be solid. You were bought with a price. Therefore, do not become a sell out to the world. Anchor your soul in the Lord. Strive for perfection each day. Press in to Christ Jesus. When the world sees you as weak, you are made strong in Christ. His grace is sufficient to keep you grounded in Him.

If you follow Christ, like palms, you will not be stunted in your growth. Never become complacent in the Lord. There are higher heights and deeper depths in Christ. Never stop advancing in the Lord. Continuously seek God and make sound improvements.

Religion and man's doctrine will no longer constrain you from following God completely. Align yourself with the Word of God. Do not worship man and neglect God. Search and study the Word of God for all truth. Once you realize God's Truth, do not be moved. Do not appear Holy, be Holy. The Lord has worked too many miracles in your life to keep up charades and façades. Christ

141

has healed you and your family. Christ lives and therefore, a religious spirit and man's doctrine has no place in daily living.

Ref: *Hebrews 2:1-4*

Take heed to the gospel that has been preached from the mouthpieces of God. Hold strong to His Word so you will not be uprooted. Do not despise small beginnings. If God can trust you with a little, He will bless you with abundance. To whom much is given, much is required. Be set in the ways of God. Exercise care and attentiveness to keeping your faith in God. Do not become preoccupied by irrelevant situations and circumstances that arise from day to day. Be steadfast in your prayer life. Situations and circumstances should not move you; you should move and transform them by the power and authority of Jesus Christ. God is glorified when you give His Word back to Him. He activates heaven to move on your behalf. Know this fact and, hence, be not moved by the world.

Heavenly angels are assigned to you. These angels war on your behalf. Therefore, continue to pray and fast so that they can continue to fight spiritual wickedness in high places. Wait on the Lord for your blessings. Be not discouraged because the prince of Persia is waging war to prevent your blessings from being delivered. Know you are victorious in the end and you will not be moved. Rejoice regardless because the fight is fixed and you win. There is no need to doubt or to be disappointed. Be righteous in your asking. Be sincere. Know that the blessing is on the way. Be because "I AM" is!

There is nowhere to hide from the Lord. At all times be aware that God is Omnipresent. He sees all and knows all. The Lord said in His word that He would not tempt you beyond what you were able to withstand. God is the Tester. Satan is the tempter. Know that God allows Satan to tempt you. You possess the secret weapon, however, which is the Word of God. Pass the test because you are grounded in Scripture. Become like Jesus when He was tempted. Firmly state, "It is written." Do not allow the devil to shake you. You are blessed to have Job experiences. God has asked Satan, "Have you considered my servant (insert your name here)." This means that God finds you to be upright. The Lord knows that you will not curse Him. The Father knows that you will bear false accusations. There is always a But God in the midst even though you will grieve by a loss of possessions. God will restore unto you that which was lost and you shall receive a double portion.

So stand erect like a palm. Remain unmovable. Remain anchored. You are a permanent fixture in the Kingdom of God. Neither life, nor death, nor principalities should separate you from the love of God.

Moving in Time

> To every thing there is a season, and a time to every purpose under the heaven... I know that, whatsoever God doeth, it shall be for ever: nothing can be put to it, nor any thing taken from it: and God doeth it, that men should fear before him. *Ecclesiastes 3:1, 14 KJV*

You are now arriving in a place in your life where you should realize that a set time has been determined to move in the Kingdom. There is a time and place for everything God said in His Word to come into BE-ing. God has foreordained every moment that comes forth out of the future into the present. God framed the worlds. He thought and spoke things into existence because He knows the beginning and the end. It is your responsibility to move beyond the cross, become a permanent fixture in Christ, and know the divine timing of God.

Know that God appoints seasons for everything. He moves according to His wisdom because He knows how things will turn out. You must be obedient and engage Him. There is no Big Bang Theory. God spoke and the earth was formed. Do not rely on science to prove or disprove the movements of God. Science deals in theories and God's people deal in Truth. Nothing occurs without the power of God. Everything has supernatural timing decreed by God in His infinite wisdom.

Recognize that God knows the conditions of His people, His church, and the world. He knows when you are suffering and He knows when you are flourishing. God knows when to send His representatives to lift you up. He also instructs them to prepare you for His next move.

Move with purpose. Grasp the concept that when brethren do not move in time; God chastises, afflicts, or allows death to accomplish His will. God will also prune the unproductive from His Vine. You are plugged into God with every breath you breathe. Always move forward with Godly productivity. God delights and takes pleasure in you following Him in season and out.

> **A time to be born, and a time to die; a time to plant, and a time to pluck up that which is planted. *Ecclesiastes 3:2 KJV***

You can never find the right time to act because your thinking, if not spiritual, is flawed. Your days in the Lord are numbered. You know when you started the journey because you know when you were born. However, the end is only known by God. He moves according to the length of time given. You are destined to be born in His timing. You are preordained to die in His timing. This knowledge may seem contrary but God is in total control. You cannot pass your time limit in Christ. The day turns into night and the night turns into day. There is perfect timing. Seasons change in perfect timing. Plant when the season is right. Wait for the harvest and then pluck up that which was planted. You are a sower. In every season there are plants to sow; you should always be planting God's Word according to the season. God is constantly watering planted seeds. He shines His light on those saplings to help the growth process. He even gives instruction on when to cover and protect the plants. Be punctual in God's timing and purpose. Every hour is fixed. Do not put off today's assignment until tomorrow. The perpetual cycle of procrastination will never allow you to catch up to God's timing. You should never disappoint God. He planted purpose in you. He expects that you operate in divine purpose. In God you should live, move, and have your being.

A time to kill, and a time to heal; a time to break down, and a time to build up. *Ecclesiastes 3:3 KJV*

You are a soldier in the army of the Lord. The Lord God says in His Word that WHEN you go out to battle that you are not to be afraid of their (the enemies) faces. He said He would be with you. When you are on the battlefield you are expected to kill. Kill utilizing the Word of God. This is how every battle fought for the Lord is won. The art of war lies in God fighting the battle. In His Word, He declared that vengeance was His. Every evil seed that has been planted is killed with the Word of Truth. You will incur wounds while on the frontline and God knew it. But, He did not predestinate you to be the walking wounded. This is why there is also a time to heal. Take time to mend. Your weapons are not carnal but mighty through God to the pulling down of strongholds. You must make a joyful noise unto the Lord in order for the walls of Jericho to come tumbling down. Once you have conquered the enemy's domain you must build up the land. Holiness must be installed and implemented in the land. Move to kill according to the Truth because no weapon formed against you shall prosper. You are healed by His Word because by His stripes you are healed. You are to tear down and build up because you are a restorer of paths to dwell in. You are a repairer of the breach according to Isaiah 58:12.

A time to weep, and a time to laugh; a time to mourn, and a time to dance. *Ecclesiastes 3:4 KJV*

Mourn with those who mourn because there will come a time when someone will mourn with you. Weeping only endures for a night but joy comes in the morning. The children of Is'rael wept when they were in captivity and they rejoiced when they were released from it. Laugh because it is good for you. Medically speaking when you laugh it gives your inner parts a good workout. The Bible declares that a merry heart does good like a medicine. Sing because you are happy. Rejoice because the Lord is your Salvation.

Through the good and bad, sing, dance, and shout unto the Lord. Dance as Da'vid danced. It does not matter who looks on you, dance.

Even the order in which to display your emotion is in God's timing. You weep before you laugh. Mourn before you dance. You sow in tears and your harvest is joy.

> A time to cast away stones, and a time to gather stones together; a time to embrace, and a time to refrain from embracing. *Ecclesiastes 3:5 KJV*

Stones have been cast at you by the enemy. These stones were meant to be stumbling blocks. At the appropriate time you must cast these stones away so they do not hurt or harm you. At other times, you are to take those very stones and turn them into a fortress. Build houses with them. Recognize that sometimes the stones you are casting away are the ones who reject Christ as their Lord and Saviour. Consequently, the stones that you gather are the converts to Christ. All stones serve a purpose in its appointed season. Be wise in knowing what to do with individual stones in the season at hand.

Friends mean well but they will not always understand where you may be in life. When friends show they are faithful and push you into destiny, you embrace them with open arms. They are divine inspirations. Appreciate the cheering squad. As soon as suspicion arises and friends are deemed unfaithful or unworthy of trust, you must refrain from embracing them. They will become hindrances to the forward momentum you are building in Christ. Also treat your loved ones and family members with the same mentality.

It is all about Godly sanctification and consecration to the Lord. God will let you know when to embrace and when to refrain. If you do not take heed to His timing, then you walk in disobedience unto Him. The Bible declares that you should abhor the presence of evil and cleave to that which is good. God in His timing will tell you which is which. Seek discernment of good and evil from the Holy Spirit. Do not allow your emotions to rule just because you have to refrain from embracing those you care about. With obedience comes submission. Live life with purpose!

> A time to get, and a time to lose; a time to keep, and a time to cast away. *Ecclesiastes 3:6 KJV*

God will always provide divine timing to seize perfect opportunities; from money, to good deals, to excellent interest rates, and on and on. When you are faithful to God, He will assign a season of favor in your life. During this season of favor, God desires you to operate in His wisdom, knowledge and understanding. God wants you to remember His Word about the ant so that you are not the sluggard. You must gather your meat in the summer. You must not ignore wisdom in storing up provisions. God teaches you to do this even in your season of getting. With getting comes losing. The world system teaches that there will be stock market crashes, bad economics, and what have you, but as a Christian who is an ambassador for Christ, you have the wisdom to store up meat. Understand that the Lord gives and the Lord takes away. You should not be affected by world economics or the stock market. Trust and believe in a higher source which is always God the Father. Christ is your Jehovah-jireh. The Lord is your provider, not the world.

The five wise virgins and the five foolish virgins are great illustrations of a time to keep. If the wise virgins gave their oil to the foolish ones, they would have missed the bride groom as well. It is important to know when to hold onto what you have. That does not always mean you are stingy. There is a difference. God will instruct you at times to keep your possessions, your advice, your finances... Faith without works is dead. Consult God to determine if you should give or keep. If He says to keep then do not feel guilty. Why feel guilty when you are walking in obedience to God.

Become aware of God's shift and timing for casting away things in your life. These are true walks of faith. Do not hold on to things so tightly that they run the risk of becoming idols and wicked altars. Rather than seeing you live in darkness, God will tell you to cast it away. Throwing temper tantrums is a sign that you may be setting up idol worship in your heart. Love God more than the love of whatever needs to be cast away.

A time to rend, and a time to sew; a time to keep silence, and a time to speak. *Ecclesiastes 3:7 KJV*

Know when it is time to rend or tear up certain things or wrong mindsets. When you see lost souls or brethren in the Lord going astray, make it your Godly assignment to tear up that evil cloak through prayer – stand in the gap on their behalf. God will never lead you astray when you follow Him. It is always man that backslides into a worldly nature of sin. It is your duty to tear down negative strongholds so that the captive can be made free.

There are also times of rending when you experience grief. The Jewish custom of mourning was to rend clothing. You will go through periods of grief. There is no escaping it. Sorrows do not last always, that time must come to an end. When the end comes, it is time to sew up your clothing. You must undo what you have done by way of rending your garments of sorrow and grief.

God will deem a period of silence in your life. You must take heed to your ways. You must bridle your tongue. In order to know what season you are in, you must listen to the voice of God for directions. You cannot listen if you are always speaking. Once the Lord has finished speaking, become His mouthpiece. It is your duty to let all know the time and season when the Lord says to speak. Honor God for speaking to you as well as through you. Educate others in the Glory of God.

> **A time to love, and a time to hate; a time of war, and a time of peace.** *Ecclesiastes 3:8 KJV*

You must be like your Father who art in Heaven. You must love the sinner and hate the sin. Do not shun sinners because the Father is able to save them. However, do not tolerate sin. Hate it. You must hate what the Lord hates and love what the Lord loves.

When you love, show yourself friendly and approachable to sinners. Your Holy light attracts them to you so that they may see God. Jesus fellowshipped with those classified as unworthy nobodies. You must not be arrogant to think of yourself more highly than you ought. Follow the examples of Christ.

There will come a time to hate. Recognize a time of evil familiarity that you will need to shun. Yield to the Holy Spirit and hate the evil. Do not be a part of what is going on if it does not line up with the Word of God. Realize that sometimes you must leave places.

In war, God draws His sword of judgment and gives His charge to devour all manner of evil. God calls for divine order. Anything found out of order He declares war, unsheathes His sword, and consumes all unrighteousness. When God is satisfied, He sheathes His sword to cease from making war and peace falls upon the land. War does not last always and neither does peace. Everything under the heavens operates in cycles. It is God who controls the cycles of your experiences.

Ref: Ecclesiastes 3:9-15

Ta'mar was secluded from troubles remaining in peace. This righteous spirit exemplified flourishing in spite of, remaining rooted in God regardless of the circumstances, moving according to time and season via God's instructions, and revealing the sevenfold Spirit of God. This upright spirit did not remain in a broken posture. This Godly spirit stayed erect refusing to live life downcast and brokenhearted. Ta'mar did not carry around volumes of pain, suffering, hatred, humiliation, and so forth. This honorable spirit did not go around glorifying the wrong.

The Lord is teaching you to hold on to your peace because He is fighting your battles. As a result, you will witness Am'non being slain. In the Old Testament, there were peace offerings made on the altar. Jesus Christ died for you that He may become the ultimate peace offering. You simply have to stay in His Will to exact the peace you desire to see manifested in your life.

The KJV Bible references to the word peace some 400 times. There is something to remaining in peace. God wants to convey to you the importance of remaining in His house of Peace. The Holy Spirit will comfort you. If He couldn't, He would not have said it in His Word.

In the Bible days, the priests stated, "Go in peace." Depart from evil and do well. Seek peace and pursue it at all costs. The Ta'mar Spirit seeks peace at all costs.

We read that Ta'mar remained in peace and no more was said of her life. The reason being is that Ta'mar dwelled in the Father's house who is Peace - end of the story. Ta'mar represents victorious peace.

Peace in the Old Testament means to be "complete; finished or to make whole or good." In the New Testament **Peace** is defined as "a state of tranquility; exemption from rage and havoc of war" or "security, safety, or prosperity." Both of these descriptions of peace shall become powerful in your life as you apply it. God's Glory of Peace is now revealed unto you. Use your testimony to defeat the enemy. Stand strong and be the palm ambassador the Lord has purposed you to be.

> **Father God in the name of Jesus. Lord thank You for teaching me about Ta'mar and how this upright beautiful spirit was able to remain in You in peace. Lord restore the peace in my life. Father I need a refreshing experience from on high. Lord cause me to walk, talk, eat, and sleep in peace. Lord, I thank You for fighting my battles. I now know that the battle was never mine to begin with. Thank You Lord for destroying all negative strongholds in my life that caused me to function outside of Your peace. Jesus I thank You for instilling in me a peace that surpasses all understanding and blessing me with your stronghold Lord. Holy Spirit I am now ready to transform in the safety of Your habitat. Lord have Your way and give me a deeper understanding of peace. I thank You and glorify Your name Jesus. Lord, I thank You for being my one and only Jehovah-shalom. Lord, I am now walking in peace and thanksgiving is in my heart. Father, I will keep pressing towards the mark of a high calling for my life with the peace I now have. I will never ever allow any person, situation, or circumstance to steal my joy again. I now stand on the promises You have given to me. I praise Your name God for turning my life around. Lord God, I thank You for the tranquility that is pouring over me now. I bless Your name Jesus for making me complete in You. This is Your servant's prayer. Amen**

About the Author

Minister Tiana McGlockton is a native of Tallahassee, Florida. She received her Associate in Arts degree in Public Affairs from Tallahassee Community College.

She is a dedicated member of Shiloh Apostolic Faith Church where Elder Edith W. Hall is her pastor. Pastor Hall's vision for Shiloh is the "Church of a New Generation." With this, Tiana has freely expressed a unique, boldness in the Lord. She has been prophesied to verifying that she will be able to make leaps and bounds past obstacles, reaching hurting women. In 2005, she was ordained to preach the gospel.

Tiana encountered the Lord before the age of ten years old and completely gave her life to Him in her early twenties. She loves the Lord with her entire being. The more she learns of Him, the more she thirsts after Him. She strives towards developing a Spirit of Excellence like Daniel. She often works behind the scenes sowing seeds and creating written works in various ministries. She is a humble servant of God whose only desire is to stay at His feet learning His Will for her life.

God instructed her to resign from her job in late May 2009. He has proven Himself to be her Jehovah-jireh.

In 2010, God gave Tiana U.N.L.O.C.K. Potential Ministries. U.N.L.O.C.K. stands for Unleashing New Levels of Christ's Knowledge. This ministry provides Level to Level, Dimension to Dimension, and Realm to Realm building scriptural lessons to assist the Body of Christ's growth as well as drawing lost souls to Christ. The mission of the ministry is to transform minds from "my will" to the Father's Will.

Tiana has a divine destiny that will take her many different places. She has transitioned from standing still and learning of God to hearing the Voice of God and moving according to His Will.

Contact and Booking Information:
unlockpotential@live.com

Made in the USA
Charleston, SC
24 August 2011